ON THE EDGE

Health Crisis: Helping Yourself

ON THE EDGE

Health Crisis: Helping Yourself

Peggy Maddox

Glenbridge Publishing Ltd.

Cover Design by Patricia Hobbs

Illustrations by Jennifer A. Rosen

Library of Congress Catalog Card Number: LC 90-81973

International Standard Book Number: 0-944435-11-4

Printed in the U. S. A.

To my sister-in-law and friend:

MARNEL MADDOX (1939-1989)

CONTENTS

FOREWORD

There are times in our minds and times in our lives when all seems lost. It is at these times that we find ourselves and our salvation. There are few challenges as significant as the threat to health and life.

At such times we have choices . . . choices that either turn our very essence over to others or that lead us to seize those special moments in our lives . . . to exert our greatest inner power for the ultimate in self-actualization and expression — to make a supreme personal statement . . . perhaps to live or to die but, most important of all, to dictate how we do either.

We have grown up in our culture without instructions or experience relative to dying, and precious little training about a much more crucial issue — how to *live* and *take charge* within our own psyche during a moment of crisis — particularly a health crisis.

Nowhere can one learn this better than from someone who has met such a challenge, particularly one who has met the challenge so successfully and completely. I have known many people who have faced and engaged this struggle but none with more creativity and grace than Peggy Maddox. I delight in her spirit and in her success. Join her . . . reach with every fiber of your being for all that you might have and all that you can be. Venture into the experience of self healing in a way that few have been able to describe. Bring those around you into the "aura" of self-discovery and enrichment that such a journey brings.

J. Anne Nizze, B.A., P.A.C.
John Wayne Clinic
UCLA

ACKNOWLEDGMENT

I especially want to thank my mother and father, Loretta and Ed Farrell, my husband, Dick and our sons, Larry and Chris for their inspiration, love and support.

Grateful acknowledgment is expressed to Manon Tingue for her exceptional editing; to LaVada Weir, my writing teacher, and to Mary McAdara, Joy Rosen, and Tina Saxe for their help in preparation of the manuscript.

There are a number of people who deserve thanks for their contributions to this project. I would like to name all those who gave me help when I needed it. Rather than risk omitting someone, a special thanks to each of you for your support and encouragement in writing this book and to the Insight Seminars that helped me get started in realizing my dreams.

AUTHOR'S NOTE

This book is not meant to be devoured in one reading. Rather it is to be used as a guidebook or reference book and to be consulted in dealing with various feelings and emotions when they arise.

When my mother first read the manuscript, her comment was, "There are too many things to do." You may feel the same way if you try to do everything suggested. At various times during my recovery I tried many different things. I have included all of them since I have no way to measure your individual preference.

My hope is that by reading this book it will make you aware of the strength of your *inner spirit* and that you will learn to call on it. Once you start, you will find it is your lifesaver, the resource you have been given to help overcome fear, depression and anger. Use it and live with peace and joy.

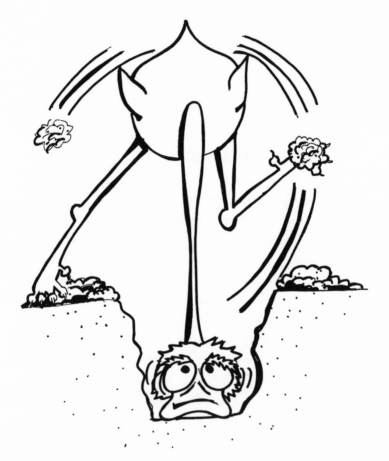

Don't Keep Your Head in the Sand

CHAPTER I

ACCEPTING THE CHALLENGE

*"It is my experience as a health doctor for
thirty years that patients must become one of
their own doctors and participate in their
recovery. Remember, health is an inside job."*
Dr. Michael McGowan, N.D.D.C.,
Wrightwood, California

MY TURNING POINT

"Why not you?"
Those three words changed my life.

One day I was talking with a friend on the telephone
about her husband, who had suffered a stroke two years

earlier. She had been bothered, she told me, that every day, as he sat at the kitchen table, he would ask, "Why me?" Finally, tired of hearing it, she asked, "Why not you?"

After our conversation ended, I knew I would always carry with me the message behind the words. I had just had my second surgery within the year for metastatic malignant melanoma. I could not look toward the future without crying. I was enraged because I was a cancer victim. After all, I was a good person; I taught health classes and lived by my teaching. How could this possibly happen to me?

At that moment, I turned from looking at my disease as a curse and turned it into a challenge. I had to get my head out of the sand, past the anger, the *"Why me?"* and look toward the future positively. I would learn to participate in my recovery and I looked forward to the challenge.

So what if I had only six months to live? What was best; to give in and accept the prognosis, or to seize it as an opportunity to improve the quality of my life and hopefully to extend it by believing that the experimental immunotherapy program I was to start would help in my recovery? Time became very precious. Suddenly, I realized that dwelling on the past was a waste of time and would only lead to depression. It was vital for me to center my thoughts on what I was going to do in the future. From that moment on, my prime objective would be to give my life direction.

None of us is given guarantees in this life; the time we have may be limited. We do have choices, though, about how we live our lives. I knew that in order to survive I would have to focus on living and being positive.

When we are confronted with a life-threatening illness, most of us feel confused, not sure which way to turn. We know we must start doing something to keep our outlook positive, even if, in the process, we may develop the "microwave syndrome," expect instant results and are thrown a curve when they don't happen. A courageous friend once described his fight against cancer by relating it to a horse race. "I feel like I am running in a horse race. Sometimes I am ahead, and there are times when it seems as if I am falling behind. I know that if I can keep ahead of it, I will win the race and survive." He was telling me he would meet the challenge and win, and that all of us need to keep our eyes on the brass ring.

Sometimes it is easy to feel defeated and that it is okay to slow down in your fight. But if you take time to look behind and keep wondering "Why me?" it can cost you valuable energy. Don't spend time asking, "Why do I have this illness?" or "What did I do to deserve this?" Keep looking forward by focusing on the brass ring — the trophy at the end.

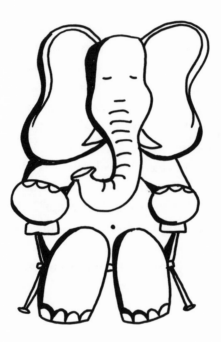

Take Time to Listen to Your Inner Voice

CHAPTER II

THINKING POSITIVELY

"Once I made my decision to have the heart transplant, I told myself it would be a success. I would have it no other way. When my diseased heart was removed, it literally fell apart. One of the doctors commented, 'The only reason he is still alive is because he wants to be.' "

George Happe, first heart
transplant patient, UCLA

It was as though the world had turned black when I first heard and, a little later, finally realized the implications of my diagnosis. Depression overwhelmed me, robbing me of any will to fight. One night, as I tried in vain to get to sleep, my mind began to wander, and I thought back to another stress-filled time in my life and how I had coped with it. Then I realized, no matter how impossible it seemed, I had to turn my thoughts around. I might not have a great deal of time left but I would live during that time, and I would not allow my sense of hopelessness to undermine my life and all those around me any longer. As I began to struggle against the weight of my negative outlook, I learned the awesome power of positive thinking.

Its importance cannot be overemphasized. Though you may not believe this at times, you are not at the mercy of people and events because *you* can control your thoughts; it's literally up to you to choose positive or negative thoughts. You can alter your perception of a situation by changing your mental attitude.

It has been statistically demonstrated that a patient with a positive, healthy attitude and a sense of humor is far more likely to overcome his disease than a patient who feels depressed. Our responses are geared to how we perceive what we see around us and how we feel about ourselves and others. How do you see yourself? People who always view themselves and life in a negative way work themselves into a state of low self-esteem and sometimes depression. The stress that accompanies negativity is a heavy burden on your physical well-being, and it may have an adverse affect on your longevity.

Remember the last time you were in a very positive, up-beat frame of mind? Recapture that feeling. Describe it to yourself. How did you feel? Confident, energized, focused, happy?

When you feel negative, how do you feel? Blah, down and out, tired? Take a minute now and think about how you are feeling. If you are able to say whether your spirits are up or down, you are able to practice self-awareness, and this is your first step forward. If you feel you could say you are at the lowest point of your life, it's good news. Once you realize you have hit bottom, the only way to go is up.

Every time you envision the worst, your body becomes tense as it reacts to the situation. Your "fight-or-flight" instincts are called into action. Your adrenaline flows, and your pulse quickens. If you dwell on destructive thoughts, you will soon exhaust yourself mentally, emotionally, and physically. Negative thinkers frequently suffer from stress-related physical ailments such as headaches, gastrointestinal problems, and high blood pressure. You can help restore your balance by changing negative thoughts into positive thoughts.

There are many avenues leading to creating and holding on to positive thoughts and keeping negative moments at bay. As a start, learn to apply an immediate remedy. When a negative thought overtakes your conscious mind, stop, take a deep breath, pause for a drink of water or a warm cup of tea, and think of something that brings you joy by remembering and savoring a wonderful moment from the past. Keeping that feeling in mind, do something positive. Visit a card store and find a card for someone you haven't heard from lately. Just reading some of the cards will put you in a more positive mood. If you are walking down the street, pick up some litter you didn't discard. Take a short drive and visit a place that has a lovely, scenic overlook or put some music that you love on a tape deck. Just going for a walk can be remarkably therapeutic. Studies show that movement is one of the best ways to overcome depression, even when it's as simple as reorganizing your sock drawer or tool box.

DO AWAY WITH "WHAT IF . . . ?"

My husband suffered his first heart attack in the middle of the night. During the trip to the hospital, my mind was in turmoil. What if he doesn't make it? How would I raise our two sons, ages 12 and 8, without him? Could history be repeating itself? Our sons just happened to be the same ages that my brother and I were when my dad had his first heart attack. I couldn't focus at all. I was frightened about my husband's health, my children's future, and myself. As I sat in the emergency room, I looked up at the large clock on the waiting room wall. It was then that I realized that there was only the present moment.

There were two other families in the emergency room. One was a man waiting for the birth of his first grandchild, reading a book and trying not to appear anxious. The other family was gathering together and making phone calls. They had just lost their nineteen-year-old son in a motorcycle accident. Again, I looked up at the clock and I suddenly knew that we had no power over the hands of time. We couldn't turn the hands of time forward so that the grandfather might hold his new grandchild in his arms, nor could we turn the hands of time backward so that the grieving family could tell their son how much they loved him. We only had that precious moment.

I knew that what had happened in my past, and the "what ifs" I had imagined had no meaning at this moment. Instead, I had to concentrate on the present. I had to replace my negative worries with positive thoughts. I thought about how thankful I was that my husband was in a well-equipped hospital staffed by excellent professionals. He was getting the best possible care. I made myself recognize that the doctors caring for my husband were providing excellent treatment, and I pictured my husband responding to their care. I began to feel that he would recover, and in a little while I found myself filled with an inner peace.

DEALING WITH STRESSFUL SITUATIONS

Human beings are creatures of habit. We tend to eat at the same time every day, park in the same place, and part our hair on the same side. When our routine is interrupted, we tend to panic. The boss wants the report *now*; the car breaks down; our child brings home a failing grade. Immediately, we react with the first signs of stress; quickened heartbeats, insomnia, headaches, intestinal problems, and general anxiety.

But problems that seem overwhelming almost never are — when we give them a second look. Generally, things can be fixed. Overtime will probably speed up the report; the mechanic will fix the car; a tutor can be found for the child. Begin by thinking about how seemingly impossible situations can be fixed and then make a list of steps you can take to make things better. This method of handling difficult situations is positive. "Going to pieces" is negative and accomplishes nothing.

When a potentially threatening roadblock stops us in our tracks, we face a stressful and dangerous time. Any type of change affects our emotional structure even though we recognize "change" as a constant in life. People die, people move in and out of our lives, our financial and health situations may suddenly change, we change jobs, lose jobs, our children grow up and leave us, and so on. We must learn to accept ourselves as the only real constant. We are "whole" within ourselves, and if we are positive in our thinking and we have learned to like ourselves, we can rise above any situation. It may be difficult to keep your outlook in balance, and some days it just doesn't happen. Keep trying and you will find yourself in balance again.

Don't be afraid to confront your problems head-on or to accept change because you don't know what the outcome will be. There are no guarantees. The risks and rewards involved in positive action are as varied as the colors of the rainbow. The patient who uses an experimental cream for acne takes far less risk than the cancer patient who uses an experimental drug to treat his malignancy. The individual who invests in a blue chip stock takes far less risk than the person who invests a dollar in a lottery ticket. Yet, all these individuals have shown positive action. They have been optimistic. To take no action at all would definitely result in no reward. Positive action begets the possibility of success and the emotional growth associated with it.

LOVE AND LAUGHTER

Love is our most positive emotion, and laughter is our most positive action. The more you love, the more you laugh, the better you feel.

Share your love and laughter with everyone you meet. Help to brighten their day and in so doing brighten your own. Smile at the tired cashiers in the supermarket and compliment them on something. The odds are strongly in your favor of getting a smile back. Tell the harassed mother with a crying baby, "They always get cranky at the most inconvenient times, but aren't we lucky to have them?" Giving positively to others gives you a warm feeling inside. Remember the person you reminded that human beings care for each other may carry it with him through the day and pass it on to someone else. You could even start an epidemic of smiles.

SURROUND YOURSELF WITH POSITIVES

Through bad days as well as good, you need to keep your spirits up. You are always susceptible to your surroundings, other people's moods, and the myriad factors that can raise havoc with your outlook and with your immune system. If you are ill, these positive suggestions may be helpful:

- *People — listen only to good news.* When family and friends tell you of others worse off than you, stop them in mid-sentence and ask them to tell you about someone who has had a good experience. Request that they hold the horror stories until you have recovered. Tell them that uplifting thoughts and experiences have a positive effect on your immune system and that, as part of your healing process, you are only allowed to think in positive ways.

- *Media — watch only positive TV shows.* If you are watching a show and something comes on that upsets you or that you know will affect you in a negative way, turn it off or change the channel. I enjoy watching the *Three Stooges* or shows that before my illness were too slapstick for me — I needed to get my tickle bone tuned up, and this did it. If you are dissatisfied with TV programming, then rent uplifting and funny movies to play on your VCR.

- *Reading — skip depressing newspaper headlines and articles.* How do you feel after reading the newspaper? If you are depressed, then avoid reading it. Read only those parts of the newspaper that leave you feeling undisturbed. If anything earth shattering happens, someone will tell you. Before going to bed, read some uplifting positive message. It then has all night to give positive input to your immune system.

Have the Courage to Appreciate Yourself

SELF-APPRECIATION

"I am my own best teacher. There are three things I always carry with me — the master key of love, the flaming sword of detachment, and a coat of armor that cannot be pierced."

Arlyne Waller
San Pedro, California

If you are physically under par, it is not easy to keep on "liking yourself" because you both hate and resent your affliction. That, in turn, can tend to make you begin to "hate" yourself. To counter any negative thoughts about your self worth, make a list of positive things about yourself. Place the list where you will see it often — tape it on your bathroom/ bedroom mirror or on your refrigerator, and put a copy in your car. If you are a private person or hesitant about others seeing your list, put it in the top of a drawer you open every day. When you look into the mirror, think about your assets and realize they belong to the face you see there.

During times of stress, we can forget how to live with ourselves. That's why it's so important to learn to like ourselves. You may be able to say that you love yourself and that's great but you need to both like and appreciate your-self. You are the only one of "you" in the entire world.

STRESS MANAGEMENT

Stress signals tension to the brain. The body is put on "red alert." Muscles tense, organs overreact, the heartbeat quickens, extremities tremble, and the increase of blood flowing through your body creates pressure, causing head and muscle aches, cramps, disorientation, and a feeling of lightheadedness. To fight a serious illness, it is important to learn to relax and not allow stress to drain the vital energy needed by the immune system to cope with disease. To this end, many doctors are encouraging their patients to practice visualization, relaxation, and imagery techniques as part of the recovery process.

The idea that a positive, happy attitude can be a useful weapon against a serious illness or stress may be a new concept to a great many people. However, in reality, mothers have been using mind power and positive thinking on their children for centuries. A mother will "kiss" away a cut or bruise, and the child's tears disappear. Or she will put her hand on her child's abdomen and say, "Just put that nasty tummy ache in Mommy's hand, and I'll throw it away." Miraculously, the child feels better. Through the ages, mothers have been using relaxation methods such as rocking, caressing, and singing to put their crying children to sleep.

Today, stress management classes using visualization and relaxation techniques are being offered to employees in the work place. To practice visualization you form an image in your mind of yourself performing a particular feat. Employees use this technique as a means of accomplishing their personal and professional goals. They imagine themselves interacting positively with their coworkers and doing the work necessary to arrive at their goal. The results have been increased productivity, less absenteeism, and improved employee relations. Team coaches also take full advantage of visualization techniques when they tell their players to picture themselves throwing a fantastic pass to a receiver or making a winning tackle. The player who can envision himself a "hero," often becomes one.

While visualization itself is a valuable technique for encouraging the body's immune system to work a little harder, it can be doubly effective when combined with relaxation exercises that are designed to release the body and the mind from the tension associated with stress.

I have found the following relaxation techniques very helpful. Either lie down flat or sit in a comfortable chair with a backrest in a quiet room. Wear loose-fitting, nonrestrictive clothing and no shoes. Close your eyes and breathe in through your nose. Let your breath fill your abdominal cavity and move up into your chest. Now slowly let it out through slightly parted lips.

As you continue to breathe in through your nose and out through your mouth, begin to tense specific muscles in your body then relax them. Start by tensing, then completely relaxing your feet. Continue these tensing and relaxing techniques as you work up toward your calves, your thighs, your buttocks, your back, your arms, your shoulders, and your neck, constantly breathing slowly in through your nose and out through your mouth.

When you are completely relaxed, imagine yourself in a place where all is comfortable and secure. I often pretend I am sitting next to a stream in a forest or lying in a hammock looking up at the clouds. Wherever you choose, put yourself there. Feel your surroundings and be a part of them. Keep breathing in through your nose and out through your mouth.

Next, picture how you can change or control the negatives in your life. Use a technique called imagery to draw pictures of what you are imagining either in your mind or on paper. For example, if you want to boost your immunity against the common cold, sketch a drawing of your white blood cells combatting the virus. Don't get caught up in trying to make "brilliant" mental or pictorial images though.

Whatever you choose to imagine is personal and will not be shared with anyone.

No matter how serious or trivial their malady, people can benefit from imagining the immune system as warriors, defeating the invader as in a Pac Man game. I used mental visualization as I went through my daily routines, and I had fun creating the images. While working in my garden, I imagined I was destroying any stray cells when I weeded my flower beds. When I was fertilizing my plants, I thought of the nourishment I was giving my body.

You can use these visualization techniques anywhere at anytime. In the shower, visualize the water cascading over and through your body, washing the bad cells down the drain. I love to swim, and while in the pool, I imagine all my body energy being drawn up to the sun, being churned and purified, and returned through the top of my head in the form of a white light. This reenergized feeling flows through all the parts of my body, cleansing them and leaving them in perfect form.

On special occasions, while enjoying a glass of wine or sparkling water, I feel the liquid washing through my body destroying cancerous cells. You can check the library for books describing the body to help you use visualization. The creative possibilities are endless.

REWARD YOURSELF

*"To treat yourself as your own best friend is
to open one more pathway to healing."*
Olive D. Euler, R.N.
Rancho Palos Verdes, California

Several times a day, give yourself a reward. This is not, as some of us have been conditioned to believe, a selfish act; instead, it's a powerful act of self-affirmation.

When you have changed a negative thought into a positive one, you deserve a reward. When you can say, "I am in charge of how I feel, and I am making a difference with the steps I am taking to maintain control over my life," you have made a great stride forward. You did it. You are in control of your life. Stop and take time to appreciate yourself.

Some of the rewards I enjoy most are time alone to sit and daydream, eating a chocolate chip cookie, soaking in a hot bath, going to a neighborhood or professional ball game, or just watching a bird in flight.

SUMMARY

- Don't allow negative thoughts to control your outlook.
- Focus on the here and now — don't allow yourself to dwell in the past or fear the future.
- Avoid stress — take positive steps for dealing with stressful situations.

- Be willing to accept change — remember that change is a constant in life.
- Don't be afraid to take a calculated risk.
- Share your love and your laughter by brightening someone else's day.
- Surround yourself with positives — be aware of what you read and listen to.
- Learn to love and appreciate the uniqueness that is "you."
- Be aware of your feelings and what you can do to keep them positive.
- Learn techniques for managing stress: Visualization — Relaxation — Imagery — Laughter.
- Practice mind over matter.
- Reward yourself for any progress you have made.

CHAPTER III

DEALING WITH FEAR, DEPRESSION AND ANGER

"How would you react if you were told that you had a deadly disease? Peggy Maddox faced that situation six years ago. Her response to the life threat was admirable. This handbook should be an inspiration to us all."

Joseph D. Weissman, M.D.
Clinical Professor, UCLA

CONQUERING YOUR FEARS

When you are first told you have a life-threatening illness, you react with an assortment of wild emotions — panic, numbness, disbelief, anger, and grief. Doctors know these are all normal reactions but you don't.

You replay your visit to the doctor over and over again in your mind; diagnosis, treatments, therapies, possible surgeries. The medical language itself is mind-boggling, and you find it hard to understand everything the doctor is saying to you, and you respond with questions like, "What is going to happen to me?" "Will this treatment be painful?" and "Will there be side effects?"

You feel hopelessly trapped in a situation that is out of your control and you would like to run away from it all. If only you could wake up and find it is just a bad dream! But it is not a dream; it is real, it is happening to you, and it is frightening. Suddenly, all your fears surface at once; your fear of dying, of pain, of recommended treatments, of the future, and of the unknown.

You remember horror stories and tragic television shows you have seen. Now it is happening to you. You are the lead character, and you want out. It doesn't seem fair; you are not prepared for this. Your life was running so smoothly and now this! Talk about being hit by a tank!

Many patients, longing for the reality to disappear, say to their doctor, "Just give me a shot so I won't know what is happening." If you are feeling like this, you are not alone. You are just experiencing what is known as the "fight-or-flight" syndrome.

FIGHT OR FLIGHT

Human beings have developed a complex response to impending danger known as the "fight-or-flight" response. The crackle of twigs would put primitive man on instant, emergency alert. He was ready to take on whatever was out there or, if it was too big, to turn tail and run. Whichever alternative he chose, all that built-up tension was completely drained out of his system by the time he was through. "Stress is not new. What's different is our lifestyles; cave people ran; twentieth century people sit and stew." (Emrika Padus, *The Complete Guide to Your Emotions and Your Health*, Emmaus, Pa.: Rodale Press, 1986.)

When you are consumed with fear, you can't focus; you lose perception of what's happening, you feel drained. But you can restore your energy and your focus by taking steps that will give you control of your own thoughts.

MY FEARS

I remember talking with my physician the day after my second surgery. I was groggy from the anesthetic, angry and distraught because they had found more cancer. The new experimental program of immunotherapy, that he thought might be beneficial for me, was frightening to contemplate. I remembered only part of what he said, since I was in shock and only half present mentally. But it was not until I had returned home and had time to think, away from the machines and business of the hospital setting, that the fear started to overwhelm me. I felt as though a giant bulldozer was bearing down on me. I wanted to lie down and let it steamroll over me. The more I thought about it, the more upsetting it became. I was also consumed with anxiety because I didn't want those around me to know how terrified I was.

Well-meaning family and friends told me how strong I was. "Don't cry — think positive." The same words I had said to others in their time of crisis kept coming back to haunt me.

When that fear started to rule my life, how I wished I had learned not to suppress my feelings. Now, I know that stifling or blanketing fear only makes it worse. I know it is okay to cry, and I find myself crying at the oddest times. While driving the car or looking at a loved one sleeping, I suddenly feel overwhelmed and cry. But that's all right; in fact, it's good. Tears are one of the body's ways of carrying away toxins produced during emotional shocks. Perhaps that is why we feel better after we cry.

TAKING CHARGE

My first step toward conquering my fears was to participate actively in my healing process. I started by doing research on my disease and getting several other opinions. This process gave me some answers. But beyond that it gave me the feeling of being in charge of my life. After I had decided on what treatment path I was going to follow, I could then focus on how I was going to handle the emotional part of the process.

Wouldn't it be great if we could put our bodies on automatic and go through the treatment steps that are prescribed without pain or fear? Unfortunately, we aren't made that way. We need to heed our feelings and to listen to what they are trying to tell us. They are real.

YOUR TREAT DAY

Most of us are apprehensive about visiting a doctor's office for a checkup. When the visit is for a specific procedure or some form of treatment, apprehension deepens. The word "treatment" can be threatening. Everyone has heard horror stories from friends and acquaintances about medical treatment. In fact, everyone loves to tell horror stories. There are stories about childbirthing experiences, root canals, broken arms, and so on. Take these stories for exactly what they are, "horror stories," possibly exaggerated for effect. Perhaps, though, your fear is just a fear of the unknown. Uncontrolled fear can affect the mind, and ultimately, the general well-being of the body. Your attitude in handling this uncontrolled fear or apprehension will make all the difference in the quality of your life.

Often, changing one word in a sentence can completely alter the meaning of the sentence. If you think about this and apply it to whatever you have to do that day, it can shift the way you feel. For instance, change the words "treatment day" to "Treat Day" and see what happens. When you think of your treatment day as a Treat Day, it sends the message that you are treating yourself to health and wellness. This may sound like playing a mind game but the mind is where feelings and apprehensions develop. We have to start by correcting our thinking. Try it! Whenever you go for therapy or treatment, remember that this is your day to treat yourself to good health.

Another way to improve the day still further is to invite a friend to go along with you on your visits to the medical center. Have lunch together and share the time. Then the day becomes one that provides emotional support as well as an opportunity to nourish your body and allow it to continue the process of healing. Talking with and even sharing your feelings with a friend over lunch can be good therapy and will help you release your feelings of fear and anger. A good friend suggested this idea to me at a point when I needed all the "treats" I could get.

After I had surgery to remove melanoma cancer cells, my doctor at the UCLA Medical Center told me that I was a possible candidate for an experimental vaccine, an immunotherapy program. No human had ever taken part in this program. When I was asked if I would like to participate, I was frightened and dreaded having to make the choice. Should I participate in a program that offered me hope but no guarantees and held the danger of unknown side effects? Or, should I do nothing, as some doctors suggested, and hope that they had removed all traces of this killer cancer?

On reviewing the alternatives, I chose the immunotherapy program. Since this program was experimental, there was a protocol that I had to follow in order to participate. Consequently, I had to drive a distance to receive a monthly vaccine at the John Wayne Cancer Center at UCLA. The vaccine was to stimulate my immune system. Additional blood tests between treatments would monitor my progress. To say the least, I was apprehensive.

As the time approached for my vaccine injection, my emotions vacillated from very high, when I thought I could conquer this disease, to very low, when I considered the odds against me. As I struggled to get my emotions under control, I started to write down my turbulent thoughts and was amazed to find how much it helped stabilize the emotional extremes I was experiencing. But I still had to face the reality of the actual treatment and its potential consequences.

A very close friend, who was also a good source of emotional support, drove me to UCLA for my first treatment, suggesting that, if I was up to it after the treatment, we turn this day into a Treat Day with lunch at a Beverly Hills restaurant. I began actually looking forward to the day, and that morning I put on my favorite outfit. I wanted this vaccine to be successful. I dressed for success!

This was a great beginning for me. I found there are many ways you can treat yourself. One is to buy yourself a gift. After my first vaccination I realized I had taken a big step on the road to recovery. As a reward for my bravery, I decided to buy myself a present — a treat to help celebrate my life and the positive steps I was taking to preserve it.

Treat yourself! You deserve it! You are making your best effort to recover your health by investing your time, money, and energy. This means you are actually taking care of yourself emotionally, and that will play a big part in your recovery. You don't necessarily have to buy yourself something, but you should celebrate by doing anything that especially pleases you. Here is a list of some treats I have used. Add a few of your own.

TREATING YOURSELF

- Change the treatment day to a treat day
- Make one day of the week your day

- Take yourself to lunch
- Go to a movie
- Send yourself a card
- Get a massage
- Buy yourself a magazine
- Enjoy a horse race
- Drink your morning juice from a fluted champagne glass
- Take a luxurious bath, turn off the lights, light a candle, and play soft music
- Buy yourself a single flower
- Have your shoes shined
- Use your best china for everyday meals
- Curl up with a good book
- Take a friend to lunch
- Attend a play
- Go to a bingo game
- Visit a museum
- Take time for a walk
- Go to the beach or park
- Sign up for a class you have wanted to take
- Hire a cleaning lady
- Go to a ball game
- Buy a magazine subscription
- Go on a picnic
- Hire a gardener
- Feed the animals in the park
- Buy yourself a cozy warmup suit
- Go out with a group of friends to do something crazy
- Start a new hobby

•   Eat an ice cream cone

Remember, you are treating yourself to health. This is your Treat Day. *You deserve it!*

QUICK FIXES

During the actual treatment, you may start feeling panicky and want a quick fix to get you through. Here are some suggestions:

Good Luck Charms: Believe it or not, a warm fuzzy can really help keep you calm and relaxed. A stuffed animal that has special meaning to you, a little teddy bear, a rabbit's foot or a special coin that fits in the palm of your hand can offer great comfort.

Cassette Player: Listen to your favorite tapes while receiving your treatments. Try self-help tapes, relaxation tapes, music tapes, or books on tapes, whatever helps to relax you or divert your thoughts.

Quick Relaxation Technique (for use during therapy): Using one hand, touch your thumb to your little finger and think about a time you felt warm and cozy. You had that toasty, secure feeling throughout your body. Now touch your ring finger and think about a time you were acknowledged for the great job you had done. Feel the glow of accomplishment wash over you. Touch your middle finger and think of a time you were on vacation. Smell the air and get in touch with the pleasure of being there. Touch your

Treat Yourself

index finger and remember a time when you were with someone you really cared about. Let that warm glow flood over you. This exercise can be used at any time to take you back to these times and places.

Projection Techniques: Think ahead to the day after the therapy or doctor's visit. Know that in twenty-four hours this will be over and that you will have taken another step toward your recovery.

DEPRESSION

During a major illness, fear and depression are our toughest emotional problems, and they seem to go together. In my case and perhaps for most of us, my fear so overwhelmed me that it took me a while to recognize that I was also in the throes of depression.

Can you remember a time when you were upset and instead of telling yourself that you shouldn't feel this way, you did something about your feelings. Maybe you scrubbed the kitchen floor with a vengeance, played a vigorous game of tennis, hacked out weeds or hit a golf ball. Maybe you poured out your feelings to an understanding listener or simply had a good cry. The result was RELIEF.

More than ever during a health crisis, you need to be able to think clearly, and this means ridding yourself of emotional baggage. The quickest route to overcoming negative emotions is to express your feelings through physical exercise or some form of creative act, such as sculpting, painting, writing or playing music. These activities can dissipate your fear, anger, and depression and allow you to think more rationally about where you want to go and where you want to direct your energies. Just the act of doing something positive will elevate your self-esteem and this, in turn, will foster an inner opposition to the voice of guilt and self-condemnation. As your anger is redirected, a feeling of personal authority begins to emerge; despair and frustration recede, hopelessness fades and alternative choices become more apparent.

HANDLING DEPRESSION

Depression is simply an imbalance in our emotional state and a signal to us that negative thoughts are in control. But depression can serve a positive purpose because it indicates that it is time for you to withdraw and study yourself. Mental stress has overwhelmed you and you need to rest. Try comparing mental and emotional exhaustion with physical overexertion. When you overexercise, your muscles become fatigued and cramped, and you realize you need to rest them.

You have to fight letting depression "take over" your psyche. Don't sink into self-pity. Stand back and sort out the reasons you feel so low. Find a pad and a pen and write down those reasons. Put the list where you can find it later and then do something else — reading the bible or a racy novel, turn on the TV, go for a walk, call a counselor or a friend. It may sound crazy but just the act of writing down your feelings is positive and will give you enough relief and energy to do something else, to enable you to focus your mind on other things.

Of course, depression can and may return. To circumvent that, try this when you are not depressed. A day or two after your initial bout with feeling low, find the list you made of your feelings before and read them. Let them overtake you temporarily, feeling the anger, pain, fear, and frustration. Cry, if you feel the need. Then tell your depression, "You have had your day —now, I'm going to get on with my life." You may not rebound on just one try. If you don't, try it again and again until you do. It is your mind's way of putting "you" in touch with "you." It's natural to become depressed from the toll treatment takes on your well-being. If you are getting therapy for loss of motor ability, you may feel debilitated afterwards, and side effects, such as hair loss or vomiting, can get you down. Tell your disease, "You may think you are winning, but you are only winning *this* round. I will win the fight!"

If the problems causing your depression are too over-powering for you to handle, there are support groups you can join — groups such as the Mended Hearts for heart patients; I Can Cope, Make Today Count, and Wellness Community for cancer patients; and stroke and AIDS/ARC support groups. Joining a support group means you will be with others who are dealing with similar problems. You may hear someone else expressing the same feelings you have had, and the other members may be able to make supportive suggestions.

It is comforting to know you are not alone. Sometimes just talking about your depression makes it a clearer reality. In telling someone else, you accept your problem as real. For example, you might be suffering quietly from severe migraine headaches and telling yourself, "These headaches are my fault because I worry too much." If you go to a doctor, however, and say, "I have severe migraines," the doctor will give you a remedy, and you will suddenly realize that the headaches are "real." Whatever their cause, they are real headaches that can be dealt with. You have taken "positive action" and now you are free to think "positive thoughts" without the burden of guilt and self-doubt.

If you are hesitant about joining a group and think you will feel more comfortable talking about your problems on a one-to-one basis, you may wish to contact a counselor, psychologist, or a minister. There may be other deep rooted problems in your life that are making it even more difficult to deal with your current situation. Guilt can make you feel "deserving" of your illness. Loneliness and rejection can make it more difficult for you to cope. A psychologist can help you over these hurdles.

You should never feel that you have to handle your problem alone. Help is only a telephone call away.

DEALING WITH ANGER

By its very nature, a cultured, restrained society teaches its members to be in control. Parents admonish their children by telling them, "Don't talk back!" "Watch your language!" "Don't yell!" and on and on. The inevitable result is that most of us think of anger negatively. We have been programmed to feel guilty after "inappropriate behavior," and since anger is inappropriate behavior, anger becomes associated with guilt, and we hide it even from ourselves.

When I recognized why I was angry and that I could make choices about how to handle it, I made my first step in dealing with it. I realized that in the past, I had anesthetized my anger, a process that had turned it into resentment. Somehow, I would have to make my anger work for me, not against me. I was fighting for my life, and I needed as many positive items on my side as I could get. I started by becoming aware that my illness was affecting my family, my work, and my social surroundings. I had allowed anger and turmoil to pervade my life. I discovered I was becoming upset and angry if I had to ask the children twice to take the trash out, for surely they could do this small chore for me. But the reality of an illness is that, when your world is turned upside down, it has to affects others. But everybody's situation can be improved if we let family members know that illness is what has enraged us and that we know it has affected them, too.

Everyone's anger is different. Some suppress anger; some verbalize it. We each have to learn to cope with our own emotional levels.

As adults, we swallow our anger and allow it to poison our thinking rather than allowing it to act as the release factor nature intended it to be. Each of our emotions serves a purpose. Anger is the vent which allows us to release the internal pressure that builds up when we are under stress. When we try to plug this vent, we suffer the internal explosions that result.

Have you ever heard the churning, bubbling, frenzied noises coming from within a pressure cooker? These sounds are what anger sounds like inside your body as it rumbles through your stomach, gnaws at your intestines, tightens your muscles and grinds at your brain. The food inside the pressure cooker is being cooked, and its original state is being destroyed. Likewise, raw, unspent anger is cooking you and destroying the original state of your organs.

Another analogy can be made to the effect of choking. When choking, people's muscles constrict, their eyes bulge, and the brain becomes nonfunctional due to loss of oxygen. If you are choking back anger, you are creating the same bodily reactions.

We fester and simmer and, as a result, develop head-aches, gastrointestinal upsets, sexual malfunction, and a wide array of physical symptoms. If only we could learn to say, "I have had it. I feel used and abused and I don't have to be sweet and nice anymore." "Nice" is the weakest word in the English language. It has no real meaning. Learn how not to be "nice." Learn how to be honest instead. Learn how to show your anger. After a good display you will feel purged.

Stop being afraid of your anger. Be angry and say so. It's natural. Those who love you will understand and forgive, and those who don't love you will be scared out of their socks and more thoughtful of your feelings in the future. You can wind up laughing at the multiple responses to your anger.

ANGER IS YOUR SAFETY VALVE

Anger is more than just a very strong emotion. It is a bodily function. It is your built in safety valve intended by nature to act as a catharsis. In primitive times, angry cave-men used clubs. We see anger as a natural response in children who have not yet learned socialized control or acceptable social behavior. Children scream, hit, bite, kick. Animals react to their primitive instincts. When angry, they attack. But adults are trained to think before reacting, be-cause our ability to think and rationalize separates us from lower species. However, it's vital for us not to lose sight that anger should be acknowledged. Once accepted, it then can be channeled into constructive rather than destructive pur-poses.

Whenever your body is attacked by a life-threatening illness, your red alert system goes into action. Every ounce of your physical being and energy is used to combat the illness. The person with a serious disease is caught in the midst of an enormous battle. Blocked anger can be devastating both mentally and physically. If suppressing anger is harmful even to healthy people, imagine what a destructive force it is when coupled with a serious illness. Grief is a natural reaction to the news that one has a life-threatening illness, and anger is a normal part of that grief. Clearly, the patient is in the midst of an enormous battle.

LETTING GO

Letting go of anger is important, but the anger connected with grief is apt to be misdirected. It is often turned toward the doctor who has made the diagnosis, or God, or family, but most often, it is turned toward yourself. The nature of this kind of anger makes it extremely frustrating and hard to fight. If someone steps on your toe, you know where to vent your anger. In the case of anger caused by grief, there *is* no one to blame. Consequently, anger is often blended with guilt. The patient asks, "Why me?" or "What did I do?" or "Why am I being punished?"

Anger is incredibly tough to control and use wisely, as I know from painful personal experience. It's an emotion I've had a difficult time dealing with in my own life. The word anger was loaded with negative connotations in the environment in which I grew up. It was inappropriate to be angry. If I did get angry, guilt was only a half step behind.

There was virtually no appreciation of the possibility that anger could be used constructively. Actually, as far as I can recall, I never once had anyone even spend two minutes tutoring me about the positive uses of anger. I was taught to deny my anger, to pretend I had none, and to cover it up so completely that I could fool everyone, including myself. My emotional outlook and my health have undergone a radical change for the better ever since I realized the importance of "Letting Go."

CHANNELING YOUR ANGER

> *"In the midst of being angry I have found it extremely helpful to channel this energy into my work out at the gym . . . By the end my work out (and many pieces of exercise equipment later!), I have successfully dissipated most, if not all, of the anger that had previously existed . . . — and in the process, have utilized positively what might otherwise have been negative, destructive, and depleting energy."*
>
> Frank Redzich,
> Torrance, California

When we are angry, we have enormous power available to us, and when we channel that anger in the right direction, we can benefit greatly by the energy it gives us.

After my illness struck, my first questions were, "Why me?" "What have I done to deserve this?" My life was full,

I didn't need this, and I felt life was really very unfair. I had a husband and a family to care for. The thought of having a terminal illness staggered my mind. Would I live to see my sons graduate from school? Marry? Have children? As my birthday approached, I wondered if this would be my last one. Then my husband had the wisdom to say to me, "Why not celebrate the fact that you made it to this birthday?" I did just that; the celebration changed my outlook, and I was able to form a positive point of view. If your energies are focused on resentments, these energies are simply not being used for constructive purposes. Instead, the inner turmoil you are going through leads to chronic fatigue and lowers your resistance to the healing processes.

Always be aware when anger strikes. Acknowledge and verbalize it to an understanding friend or counselor, write it down, or do both. Once you recognize it, realize that anger automatically readies the body for action. This means you can make your anger work constructively — not destructively. To counteract the physical aspects of the emotion, engage in a vigorous physical activity, if your illness doesn't limit you. Unfortunately, fatigue, chemotherapy, radiation and medications can limit our ability to participate in strenuous activity, so this isn't a solution for everybody.

Be as objective and realistic as possible about the cause of your anger. Consciously set up a habitual process of positive thought to take the place of the negative thinking that sustains and accompanies resentment. Being positive has more rewards than I ever imagined. It makes your life easier and more pleasant. Your family and friends will be elated to see you more upbeat. But you have to work at it.

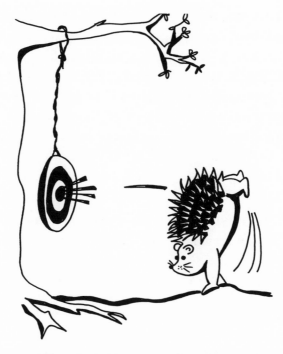

Redirect Your Anger

Remember the old song, "Accentuate the Positive"? It is a lighthearted song that makes everyone feel positive when they sing it. If you are too young to remember it, find someone who does and learn it. Make a game of it! *AC-CENTUATE THE POSITIVE!!!*

One excellent source of venting pent up anger is through writing letters. You can write a hostile, angry letter to anyone about anything. You can even write a nasty, hateful letter to your tumor or illness. Curse it, threaten to kill it (maybe you will). Remember, no one has to see these letters except you.

There are no limits on imagination. How about painting a picture of what you think your illness looks like or clipping a picture of a monster from a movie promotional ad? Paste it to a dartboard and throw your well-aimed darts at it. Talk to your disease. Tell it, "I hate you and I'll rid you from my life. I am stronger than you are." *Take your anger out where it belongs — ON YOUR ILLNESS!!!*

ANGER: What To Do With It

Below are some suggestions that can make your anger work for — not against you:

- *Cry.* It's okay to cry. Try screaming in an appropriate place, when at home alone, into a pillow, in the car with the windows up.

- *Strike out at something.* Punch a pillow or hit the mattress, buy a punching bag, go to the gym and punch their bag.

- *Vent positively.* Anger can be positive in itself. Vent your anger in aid of a specific cause. For example, write letters to your congressional representatives asking them to support research funds for treatment of your disease, or ask the FDA to approve new drugs that focus on the so-called incurable diseases. You can also write to the American Medical Association for information on experimental drugs for your illness that may not be approved as yet.

Perhaps you could even visit a children's ward and let the children know that you are sick too, that you understand that they are angry and scared. Tell them it's okay to be angry and to cry. Draw pictures of your illness, and have them draw a picture of theirs. Laugh and tell them your illness is uglier. Encourage them to scribble all over their picture and say "I hate you." Help them with their anger. You'll be helping yourself, too.

- *Record Your Feelings.* Write out your feelings. Talk into a tape recorder describing how you feel. Often by writing out the anger you will be able to release it and focus on what you really want in your life. If you feel you do not want to keep this paper around, tear it up or burn it, thereby converting the negative words into positive energy.

- *Schedule your anger.* Anger often hangs over us like a black cloud and intrudes on all our thoughts. A technique that works miraculously for me is to schedule my anger so that it does not run my life. Write your anger and your fears on a three-by-five card. Place the card on a shelf or in a drawer. Schedule a time of day for worry and anger, for example, between 8:00 to 8:15 P.M. If you find them intruding during the day, say to yourself, "I must wait until 8 P.M. to deal with this." This is an effective way of handling your time so that you — not they, have control over any of the emotions plaguing you.

- *Love Yourself.* Become your own best friend. Most of our anger is directed at ourselves. Sit down, right now, and draw up a list of your attributes. List everything you can think of about yourself — your personality, your occupation, your accomplishments, your character, your social life, your body, your mind, your relationship in the family. Don't forget your internal attributes, such as, caring, compassion, honesty, spirituality, intuitiveness, creativity, and enthusiasm. Almost everyone has attributes he/she may be too shy to acknowledge even to themselves. Be kind to yourself. When you finish the list, read it over and reflect on it often. Read it to yourself daily. Make copies of it and carry one in your wallet. Have it available so that if you start to feel down, you can remind yourself of the true person behind the shadow.

• *Talking with others.* Find a friend or a counselor, a psychologist, social worker or minister who will understand what you are going through, someone who has the time to listen. Join a support group with others facing the same challenges you are. Talking and listening are comforting, and you will realize that you are not alone. You are making a genuine contribution not only to yourself, but to the others in the support group. It is almost the best therapy there is.

SUMMARY

• Learn to confront your fears head-on
• Take charge of your healing process

- Turn Treatment Days into "Treat Days"
- Give yourself a treat
- Find ways to direct your thoughts during treatment
- Redirect your fear, depression or anger through physical action
- Learn to recognize the signs of depression
- Avoid self-pity
- Do not blame yourself
- Acknowledge your anger and learn how to channel it into constructive behavior
- Vent your emotions — cry or be angry if it makes you feel better
- Realize that your anger may be misdirected
- Learn to let your anger go
- Put your anger to work for you

CHAPTER IV

INNER RESOURCES

*"Listening to my inner voice is an excellent
reminder to me of the importance of staying
clear, focused, and open to the answers
available to me from within. That we are our
own greatest resource is a wonderful message for anyone facing a health challenge,
including people confronting AIDS and AIV
disease."*

Kim W. Hunter, M.S.W.
AIDS Program Director,
South Bay Free Clinic,
Manhattan Beach, California

How would you like to feel a surge of energy and see
the turbulence around you disappear? There is a power

within each of us that, once discovered, gives us the strength to deal with and often recover from illness. Above all, it brings us the peace we need to fulfill the gift of life. We all use this power to some degree. No one ever totally loses it; yet few realize its full potential. Many have searched for it in countless ways but few have found it because it is hidden where most of us never look — within ourselves. That power is reached by "going inside" ourselves. We reach it simply by letting go of the distractions cluttering our minds, allowing peace rather than turmoil rule us.

In our search for medical help and nutritional guidance, we look for assistance from professionals. Sometimes our stress can be handled by going within ourselves. I believe that every one of us has an inner voice that, if listened to, can give us enormous strength.

Like most of us, I had been trained from childhood to look outside myself for answers to my questions. I expected my parents and the world around me to provide solutions to my problems. I finally recognized that leaning on others for guidance usually meant my solution was at best only temporary. I spun from problem to problem, thinking that this time I would handle things better, but instead I was performing in the same way over and over again. Somehow, I had to find a way to lean on myself.

Although I didn't think so at first, the process of finding inner strength is fundamentally simple. To reach your inner voice, you must relinquish your attempts to solve problems with your conscious mind. Give up the belief that you know what has to be done and open your mind to undreamed-of horizons by becoming receptive to the strength and wisdom that lies deep within you.

The process of inner listening is not mystical, magical, or even difficult, although it may seem so to anyone new to the process or dubious about its wisdom. It takes determination and a will to succeed, but the rewards are infinite. Below are three simple steps to take to reach your inner power.

1. Realize that you cannot solve or even identify your problems with your "worldly" mind — the conscious mind that we often identify with reality.

2. Now you need to convince yourself that you have the power within you to solve your problems. You must continue to strengthen this belief until you find you are able to let go of your "worldly" or conscious efforts to solve your problems and let yourself be guided by your inner voice.

3. Calm your conscious mind; eliminate worry and its attempts to find a solution. Go beyond the harassment of conscious to the quiet and peace that lies deep within you.

My initial efforts to get through the first two steps were clouded by skepticism, but I kept on trying because a gut feeling told me I was on the right path. If I can, you can!

You may find it helps you concentrate by using a quiet place, by assuming special body positions like those used in yoga, or perhaps by the utilization of incense or candles, although none of these aids is necessary. You can simply imagine yourself as part of the vastness of the universe and join it in quiet harmony.

The first time I felt a sense of peace and power steal over me, I didn't quite recognize what had happened. Then

I knew I had found my true self and that it would guide me. I began to realize that I was taken care of, and that from then on my thinking would be clear and the actions I took would be right.

Always remember that your purpose in reaching for your inner self and attaining peace is not to be told to do something. Instead, it is to realize that you are safe, cared for, and at peace.

When we realize that a problem is not a problem but a challenge, we proceed in strength, confidence, and peace. If our strength is called into play, we will be guided and aware of what to do. We need not hurry, search, or change things. We can step back and be guided and cared for by our inner guide or the resources we have learned are there for us to draw on.

Answers come in all forms. Help is everywhere. When we quiet ourselves, put our "busy problem solver" away, go inside and open our minds — when we are at peace — the answers come in a myriad of forms. Solutions may come to us in music, painting, poetry, our loving friends, our "enemies" or strangers, everywhere we are willing to look. Answers are on billboards, in jokes, in silence, in trees, in oceans, in streams. Our "friend," our inner voice, is with us wherever we go, but we only hear and see it when we are willing.

The secret of hearing is thus a willingness to listen to our inner guide no matter what form the answer takes. I often get answers in the form of a reminder — a seemingly unrelated thought or occurrence that puts the pieces of the puzzle together.

MY INNER VOICE

When I was first introduced to meditation, I read many books on the subject but could never find the time to practice it. My excuses were always good ones. I'd decide to meditate in the backyard, away from the telephone, but when I went into the yard, I'd notice that the flowers needed watering. I find it interesting now that I could never find ten minutes for myself. My mind was always racing to get things done, and in the race I overlooked shortcuts, all because I did not stop and listen to my inner voice.

When I finally decided to get in touch with myself through meditation, significant changes occurred in my life. I became much calmer and was more focused.

Let me share with you a method that works for me. I have two favorite chairs to choose from when I meditate, one inside the house and one outside. I keep a note pad and pen next to me so that I can jot down the fleeting thoughts that go through my mind. After jotting down the thoughts, I let them go. I keep repeating a single word that is meaningful to me (I use the word "peace"). I begin to feel an inner calm, a peaceful awareness.

Once you are in the habit of reaching this inner awareness, you can do it at any time and place, even when you are harried and upset. Your mind and body remember the feeling of inner peace, and all it takes are some deep breathing exercises and your special "word" to relax you and put your body and mind in balance.

I use this technique often for short periods of time during my daily routine — while swimming laps in a pool, while doing the dishes, or while waiting for an appointment or a red light. I key into my "word" and take some deep breaths. These tools give me an immediate escape from the busy world.

Once you start listening to your inner voice, you will realize how relaxed you feel and will recognize different ways to deal with your problems.

Listening to Your Inner Voice

Our minds are very powerful and they create the world we live in. A willingness to experience is thus the main precondition for experiencing anything, including the ability to listen to our inner guide. Since our inner guide does not force us to comply, its voice is not loud and commanding. The conflicting voices of the outside world, on the other hand, seem to shriek and yell. In spite of this, they have no real power over us and operate only on the power we give them. The basis for this power is fear, and like all bullies, they try to bluster and confuse us so they get their way. As we still our minds, we come into harmony with our inner guide's direction.

To hear properly, we must want to change our perception of the world — a quite different thing from a desire to change the world. Many of our "questions" do not really seek answers; they simply call for justification of what we already believe. When we already "know" what the answer should be, how we will accept it, when it will occur, or how it is to affect us, we have closed our minds to the "real" answer, the one that is right for us.

We do not really need a clap of thunder, a holy feeling, a voice, or even a thought to gain insight. Whatever is happening now is what is supposed to be happening and is a blessing. Many of our queries are simply some form of the question, "Why is this happening to me?" We have many judgments about what should happen and what we think would be best. These judgments result from our perceptions of the world about us; they do not reflect reality, but simply a desire to control our experiences.

All of life is a learning experience. We grow and expand through everything and everyone that touches us. Cultivate this growth and learn from it. Rather than ask, "Why?" ask, "What can I do with my experience that will be fruitful and beneficial to others and to myself?" The particular form in which we hear our "voice" may be determined by our background, education, current interest, or the talents we have. Those who like to write, for example, may hear their voice best with pen in hand or at the typewriter. Others hear best while they are running, hiking, reading, painting, building, meditating, or listening to or playing music. In one form or another, the inner voice is always there, as close as our next thought.

To illustrate, suppose we consider ourselves bombarded by thousands of messages every moment, all saying the same thing but in different forms. But suppose our reception device is "turned off." To receive messages, we must first turn it on. Then, no matter what channel we're on, we will get the message in the form of that broadcast, as long as we accept that the answer is contained in that format. Its relevance to our problem depends on our willingness to accept the answer as it comes. Once you accept the answer in one form, you will see it repeated over and over in other forms until you wonder how you could have ever missed it in the first place.

Suggested below are several methods to help you to get in touch with your inner resources.

RELAXATION TECHNIQUES

> *"Being in a wheelchair and mother of three young children, I have excessive tension in my shoulders. Using relaxation techniques every day is terribly important for my physical and mental well-being. I consciously relax my shoulders and arms and visualize myself running along the beach. I picture what I want in my future — to be able to walk again."*
>
> Jan McMorran
> London, England

Here are the seven steps for relaxation outlined in Dr. Herbert Bensons's book, *The Relaxation Response,* New York: Morrow & Co., 1976.

1. Find a quiet environment free of distractions. A private room — away from telephones, street noise, and other interruptions.

2. Choose a word or phrase — a mantra — to focus on. Dr. Benson recommends the word "one." You may prefer something else, like "love" or "peace." It is more meaningful if the word has special meaning to you, but it can be nonsensical too, perhaps a sound or series of sounds that have a soothing tone. Once you pick your word, however, stick with it. In time, you will associate that word with the correct relaxation response.

3. Sit upright in a comfortable position with your hands resting on your lap.

4. Let your eyes close gently and take a few moments to relax your muscles and quiet your mind. (Sometimes a few deep breaths help prepare you for meditation.)

5. Now, breathing normally, become aware of each breath. Working with the slow, natural rhythm of your breathing, repeat your focus word or sound silently on every exhale.

6. Disregard distractions; they're not important. "A passive attitude appears to be the most essential factor in eliciting the relaxation response. Thoughts, imagery, and feelings may drift into one's awareness. One should not concentrate on these perceptions but allow them to pass on."

7. Continue this exercise for ten to twenty minutes. Use your judgment or sneak an occasional peek at a wrist-watch to gauge your time. Don't use an alarm clock since the

noise can be too disturbing. When your time is up, remain quiet with your eyes closed for a few minutes to allow your thoughts to readjust to full wakefulness.

For additional information on relaxation, check the many books in libraries and bookstores.

HYPNOSIS

All of us like to think that our actions and reactions are a result of logical thought processes, but the fact is that suggestion influences our thinking much more than logic. Consciously or unconsciously, our feelings about almost everything are largely molded by ready-made opinions and attitudes fostered by our mass methods of communication. We cannot buy a bar of soap or a filtered cigarette without paying tribute to the impact of suggestion. Right or wrong, most of us place more confidence in what "they" say than we do in our own powers of reason. We distrust our own mental processes and want an expert to tell us what to think and feel. Despite this tendency to adopt our attitudes from others, man has always been dimly aware that he can influence his own destiny by directing his thoughts and actions into constructive channels. To some extent, he has always known that his mind exerts a powerful

> *influence on his body, and that thoughts can have harmful or helpful effects on his emotional and physical health. The ancient Egyptian sleep temples and the attempts by early physicians to drive evil spirits out of the body were both attempts to influence the body through the mind.* (Melvin Powers, *A Practical Guide to Self-Hypnosis*, North Hollywood: Wilshire Book Co., 1961.)

Try a Hypnosis Class

Hypnosis is used to quiet the mind and allow only what is suggested to be noticed. After hypnosis, when the mind returns to its usual state, your thoughts retain the suggestion.

Hypnosis was a great help for me. I wanted to take the hypnosis course first so that my first experience with the cancer treatment would be a positive one. I first took a hypnosis class through adult education. These classes may be offered at community colleges. If such classes are not available in your area, you can make an appointment with a hypnotist. Interview him or her first, though, and be sure that the two of you are compatible.

Before your appointment with the hypnotist, make two lists: one list of your positive feelings or phrases you refer to in times of need, and a second list of fears you have regarding your illness. My list looked like this:

Positive

Favorite place to relax: the beach.
Favorite saying when frightened: "Let Go and Let God."
Favorite uplifting feeling: being surrounded by a pure white
    light; knowing I am the right person, at the right place,
    at the right time.

Negative (Fears)

Sun: I was afraid of the sun because I felt that too much sun
    was the cause of my melanoma (skin cancer).
Cancer: Is it still spreading?
Weak Veins: When I have blood work done or infusions, I
    am afraid the therapist will have trouble finding a vein
    that hasn't shut down. Treatments and therapies frighten
    me.

My Steps

My therapist, Julie French, used the lists I had made to
make a cassette tape. The tape is personalized, with my
name used throughout. The statement of my fears allowed
her to transform them into positive affirmations on the tape.

With Julie's permission, I have printed here my "Self-
Healing" tape. It can be used as a guideline for creating your
own tape. The approximate running time of the tape is
twenty minutes.

SELF-HEALING TAPE

"With your eyes closed, Peggy, just begin to relax. . . . Find a comfortable position and just begin to let go, let down, relaxing more and more . . . and as you begin to relax let nothing distract or disturb you. Any natural sounds that might come in, let those sounds be an indicator telling you to relax more and more. Even the sound of my voice, although you'll hear what I say clearly and be able to respond positively, the actual sound of my voice will only assist you in going to a very deep place of relaxation. . . . And now, as you continue to relax, in your mind's eye begin to visualize some sort of a container. It might be a basket or a box, something that would have a lid to it or a top to it. . . . See yourself removing the top and begin to put all of your thoughts into the container, all of your worries, concerns, anything that might be distracting, upsetting. . . . Fill up the container and replace the top and push the container off to the side so that for the next few moments your intention is totally with relaxing, with being with yourself, with healing your body. And now, as you continue to relax, begin to focus on your breath. . . . Just begin to watch the gentle rise and fall of your breath with your body. . . . With every inhalation, begin to feel yourself bringing in new energy, new life. With every exhalation, letting go of toxins, letting go of used-up energy, letting go of tightness, tension. . . . So with every inhalation you are breathing in all that supports you, and with every exhalation, you are letting go of what no longer supports you. . . . As you continue, be with the rhythmic flow of your breath. Bring your attention down now to your feet and toes. . . . Just let all the tension in your feet flow out; feel a ripple of relaxation move through your arches. As your feet relax, bring your focus up into your shins and calves, and let those muscles begin to relax. As your shins and calves begin to let go, bring your attention now up through your knees, your thighs, and up into your hips, and begin to let the major muscles in your hips and thighs let go. And as your hips and thighs begin to relax, begin to have more awareness of the surface beneath you. Trust it. Surrender to it. Let it support you. . . . And now bring your focus on up into your stomach. And let just your stomach open and relax as much as you can. And as your stomach begins to relax, allow the breath to be deeper, slower. Bring your focus now up to your chest and let all the muscles in your chest relax, and as they relax, bring your focus slowly around to your back and let all the muscles in your back begin to relax inch by inch. Let that relaxed feeling flow up into your shoulders now. And as your shoulders begin to relax, be aware of any sensations, any tingling, any change in temperature, any change in weight. Does your body feel lighter? heavier? Any of these signs are indications of you going into a deeper state of relaxation. They are all natural. So let those sensations flow now down into your arms, through your elbows, forearms, down into your wrists, hands, fingers, and begin to feel all the tension, any remaining tightness, drain out your fingertips, leaving you totally, completely relaxed. . . . And now bring your focus on up into your neck and let all the muscles in your neck begin to relax. And as your neck relaxes, let that relaxed feeling flow up into your scalp, over the back of your head, across the top of your head, down into your forehead. Let your forehead relax, all the little muscles around your eyes, down into your cheeks, down into your jaw. All of your facial muscles feel open, released, relaxed. . . . And now, just scan your entire body noticing any remaining tightness, and just breathe into it. Releasing, feeling yourself drifting, dropping deeper, deeper, deeper into relaxation. And as you continue to relax, in your mind's eye begin to picture a beach, a wonderful beach. It may be one that you have been to several times, a favorite beach. Or it may be one that you have dreamed about. See yourself a short distance from this beach. You are standing on a knoll, a grassy knoll, up several yards from the beach. There is a path that will take you down to this wonderful, sandy beach. There are wedges like stepping stones in the pathway, so that you can step with certainty and safety. There are ten steps. I'll count the steps for you, and as you step down towards your beach, with every step feel yourself letting go, letting go, relaxing, drifting, dropping, deeper, deeper, deeper into relaxation to be totally, completely relaxed by the time you get to your beach. . . . Begin now to step down. One, two, feeling so relaxed, three, four, mind and body at rest, five, six, it almost feels like floating, seven, eight, it feels so good, nine, ten, and you are now on your beach. . . . The sky is very blue, there is a gentle breeze that you can feel on your face, the waves lap gently onto the shore, and these surroundings immediately bring you a feeling of peace, serenity, and health. You feel safe and at ease with yourself. You notice that your body feels so very relaxed, your breathing is slow and even, and all of your senses begin to open up and are very acute. Take a moment and connect and tune into all that surrounds you. Breathe into you all that heals and revitalizes you. . . . Begin to walk along this wonderful beach, and as you walk, enjoy nature and all of her glory. Breathe into yourself all that is relaxing, nurturing, and healing about your surroundings. Continue to walk, and as you walk, allow your step and your breath to form an even, rhythmic pattern, so that with every step you continue to relax more and more. . . . And now see yourself sitting down on the beach, and the waves begin to lap around your feet, and as they begin to lap up around your feet and go rushing back out into the ocean, feel that each time they rush up they bring you wholeness, health, and vitality. And as they rush back out into the ocean, they draw from you all that is out of balance, all that is in disharmony, leaving you whole, complete, and healthy. Cleansing, purifying, renewing your body. . . . Continue to sit there on the beach and see that wonderful sun above your head. A golden, beautiful sun, and as it rests in the sky directly above your head, see the bottom of it opening up. . . . And you are going to send all of your energy up into the golden sun, and the sun is going to purify it, cleanse it, rebalance it. . . . bringing it back to you, sending it back to you whole and complete and healed. . . . So begin to send all of your energy up into the sun. See it whirling, churning, turning inside the sun. . . . getting balanced, recreated, renewed. . . . And now it comes back down into you through the top of your head. Let it stay in your head, down into your neck, down into your arms, the upper part of your chest, and let it touch every cell, purifying, cleansing, healing, soothing, comforting, and let it move all the way through your body until you feel healed and complete. . . . And now as you are sitting there on the beach, look and see a woman walking from the opposite direction toward you. Get up slowly. . . .and begin to walk toward her. And as you walk toward her, see that she is you, but there is something different about her. Look closely, and as you see Peggy coming towards you, begin to get a sense that she is healed, she is totally healthy. There is a sparkle about her, an aliveness about her that is very, very enticing. Walk toward her, reach out and take her hand, and as you do, feel that healthy, healed energy, that whole energy pouring into your body. . . . And you become her, you are one. And as you are one now, she begins to speak to you, telling you words of wisdom and truth. Each and every day from this day forward, I am able to heal my own body. Each day I am feeling stronger and more whole. I know my veins are strong, and I can go into my therapy and I will be fine. Each day I move closer and closer to total health. Any imbalances in my body are disappearing quickly, and I feel strong and healthy. . . . As I undergo any therapy, my body withstands it with strength and endurance, and I have only positive results. Each day I see myself free from any imbalance, and the therapy takes me quickly to total health. God's love is continually flowing through me, and I know that all I need to do is to Let Go and Let God. . . . And I know that I am the right person, at the right place, at the right time, and I am healthy, I am whole. I take care of my body, and my body responds with health and takes care of me. Each day I love myself unconditionally. I treat myself with love and respect, and my body responds appropriately. Infinite intelligence within me always does the right thing to heal my body. I can feel connected with God's healing power. It flows through me and heals me. . . . And now let that love pour through you and around you, surround you with golden light, bringing you feelings of peace and serenity and love. . . . And now it's time to come back, to return to a state of awareness and alertness. You'll leave your beach, return to the stepping stones that will take you to the top of your grassy knoll. When you get to the top, you'll open your eyes, feel totally rested, alert, and healed. . . . Moving back now towards the stepping stones, ten, nine, eight, seven, six, five, beginning to feel more awake, four, three, two, beginning to open your eyes, and one, all the way back."

BIOFEEDBACK

Biofeedback is a teaching strategy used to help people relax themselves. An instrument monitors a person's electrical activity, which indicates his or her sense of agitation or relaxation. The patient can hear, through magnified beeps, the electrical activity in the smooth muscles. When the muscles are tense, the beeps are fast, almost a continuous buzz. When the muscles relax, the beeps become slower and distinct. The machine also measures the galvanic skin response or perspiration on the skin. It measures the temperature of the fingertips, which tend to be cold when the body is tense, warmer as it relaxes. The patient can read his or her temperature on a dial, through lights, or on graphs.

With the help of a trained therapist, patients learn to relax. As the body relaxes, the patient gets immediate feedback by hearing the beeps slowing or watching the rise in finger temperature. Success with biofeedback takes a lot of practice—at home with relaxation tapes as well as in the therapist's office using the apparatus.

Norman Cousins, author of *Anatomy of An Illness,* used biofeedback techniques when working with patients at UCLA. His Psycho Neuroimmunology Task Force has completed this project with excellent results, which are recorded in his book, *Head First.*

SUMMARY

- Cultivate your inner strengths
- Learn to listen to and trust your inner voice
- Change your perception of what is happening
- Turn your experience into something beneficial to yourself and others
- Find the relaxation technique that works best for you and use it faithfully
- Tune in to your inner voice
- Try using hypnosis
- Create a "self-healing" tape and use it to overcome your fears
- Learn to use biofeedback techniques

Don't Swim in Circles

CHAPTER V

PRACTICAL TIPS

"As the owner of my own business, I have always been organized and have kept excellent business records; however, when I was faced with a health crisis after my accident, I became very scattered. Keeping a personal health record book was a lifesaver for me. It kept me focused and this, in turn, helped me regain control of my life."

Jill Sprengel, R.N.
Redondo Beach, California

It is normal to be overwhelmed by the medical information you receive during a health crisis, and it is natural that you want to do everything possible to help yourself. But don't

become obsessive about digesting every piece of medical
advice, letting it overtake your life.

STOP SWIMMING IN CIRCLES

We often seem to play the same record over and over
again in our minds. Our thoughts and ideas chase themselves
round and round. In the book *Thoughts Are Things* (California: Science of Mind Publications, 1967.) Ernest Holmes
and Willis Kinner state that:

> With regularity the same pattern of thought keeps
> repeating itself with no end in sight. And the tune
> being played is one that we definitely don't like.
> It is said that a neurotic thought pattern usually
> involves feelings of hate, fear, anxiety and guilt.
> If there is such a thing as perpetual motion, it
> exists when we find ourselves caught in the
> merry-go-round of our own negative thinking.

When we dwell on the same thought by the hour, we become
emotionally and physically drained. But we can do with our
minds just what we would do with our record player or tape
recorder — we can change the record or tape.

There are many mental records we can play that are
enjoyable and beneficial. But it takes time to discover them,
and we have to work at it. The record or tape that plays hate
needs to be replaced with one of love; fear with confidence
in oneself; anxiety with faith; and guilt with forgiveness.
When we discover that our minds are playing a negative
thought pattern, we can automatically change it and play a

more harmonious one. When we find we are not enjoying a television program, we change the channel. The same choice can be exercised in our thinking patterns.

YOUR LOG BOOK

As your doctor discusses the diagnosis and available options with you, your mind seems to shut down. Often in stressful situations, you may not be fully aware of what is happening. Confusion and fear reign supreme. A feeling of detachment from your surroundings is common. Because you are under extreme stress, you sometimes forget the names of important medical terms and diagnoses and often misplace vital information. All that needs to be done is overwhelming — informing your family and friends, scheduling appointments, or changing your business and social commitments. There are so many things to do and so little time; it is very easy to become disorganized and discouraged. But don't let yourself give up! Know that you can do it all, and that every effort you are making toward recovery will make you feel better about yourself and those you love.

Starting a record or log book is a good way to save yourself some worry at a time when you already have more stress than you can handle. I cannot overemphasize the importance of writing things down and keeping a record of names, addresses, telephone numbers, instructions, appointments, and information passed on to you by your doctors and friends. So often this information is misplaced or lost just when you need it most. Writing everything down and keeping it in one place will help relieve you of the pressure of trying to remember the overwhelming number of details that must be dealt with.

COMPACT NOTEBOOK

A five-by-seven inch notebook that can be carried in a purse or briefcase is ideal for this kind of record keeping. You will want to take it with you everywhere. Reserve different sections for the various kinds of information you need to keep. One section should be reserved for the names, addresses, and telephone numbers of doctors, specialists, and other important people you need to contact. Another section should be set aside for recording appointments and important dates. Additional sections can be used for keeping track of your medications and therapy treatments, of important questions to ask the doctor or therapist, and of information gathered about your specific illness and passed on to you by your friends and relatives.

It is also a good idea to reserve a section for personal information such as your previous health history, the names and telephone numbers of previous doctors you have visited, insurance information, social security number, driver's license number, and the names, addresses and telephone numbers of your nearest relatives. This information will come in handy when filling out the patient information forms of a new specialist or hospital.

You might even wish to include a section on personal and financial planning where you could jot down the names of books and articles you might like to read.

Don't forget to include the names, addresses, and telephone numbers of close friends and family when making up your log book. It is amazing how easy it is to forget a known telephone number or address when you are under stress.

Handy Reference

Keeping your logbook up-to-date is a great way to help you regain control of your life. In addition to providing a central location for all the important information you have already accumulated or will be gathering in the future, writing it down also makes it easier for you to remember important facts. It provides reminders about whom you have promised to call or to whom you want to send thank-you notes.

When you return home, relatives, friends, and neighbors will want to know the results of your visit to the doctor. They will be anxious and concerned and will want to help in any way they can. This help often comes in the form of firsthand experiences, treatments they have heard about, the names of specialists they feel might be of help, and the names of other people they know who have experienced what you are going through.

It is important that you keep a record of this information for future reference. Don't allow yourself to fall into the habit of writing things down on the back of an old envelope or scraps of paper. You will end up spending many frustrating hours searching for this information just when you need it most. Keep your logbook by your telephone when you are at home and in your purse or briefcase when you are away. If someone calls with information he or she thinks might be useful, don't disregard it. Make a note of it in your logbook. Information that might not seem important to you today may end up being very useful in the future.

If you meet someone in the doctor's office who has a similar illness, make sure you get his name, address, and telephone number and keep it handy in your logbook. Other patients who are experiencing the same treatments and emotional highs and lows that come with a life-threatening illness can be a great source of information and support. It is always comforting to know that you are not alone, and that you can talk with someone who truly understands your feelings.

Record Visits To Doctors; Therapies Recommended

Begin your logbook as soon as possible and take it with you when you visit your doctor's office. During your initial visit or when you are told the diagnosis, however, you may not be able to take notes or remember everything the doctor tells you. At this stressful time, take along either a trusted friend or relative who can take notes or take along a tape recorder. Although you will be aware of the words being spoken, the shock of the crisis may cause your mind to blank out and prevent you from digesting the true meaning of his words. Your mind has questions of its own, such as, "Why me?" and "How long do I have to live?" which may prevent you from concentrating on your doctor's explanation. Therefore it is important that you have some means of recording the conversation so that you can review it later.

The Log As A Focal Point

Let your logbook become the focal point for your recovery by using it to focus on your feelings. Suppose that one day you feel good about your chances of recovery, but the next day you feel that all hope is lost. It is important to identify where these feelings are coming from. Perhaps you can avoid these situations that drain you of the will to live. Just a few words in your logbook each day can help identify the situations that should be avoided, or, if they cannot be avoided, help you prepare yourself mentally for handling the situations in a more positive way. It will also be helpful in pinpointing your sources of strength so that you can draw upon these resources when you need them.

My Personal Log

My own logbook is much more than just an appointment book or a place to keep notes; it is my security blanket. I carry it with me or, if I'm home, place it by the telephone or on the nightstand beside the bed at night. In the morning it provides the details on how I should schedule the day's activities. It is my focus on life, and it has become a personal record of my struggle for survival. I like to plan well into the future and to record these plans in my logbook so there will always be something for me to look forward to. When I feel overwhelmed, it allows me to focus on one day at a time,

thus providing encouragement. As each day passes, it becomes a day of personal triumph. As I look back over all my
accomplishments, I see that I have written new chapters for
my life; each new day holds untold riches as I look forward
to new experiences and friends that will add even more
chapters.

KEEPING A RECORD BOOK

Sections for Your Record Book

- *Personal:* Information you need for filling out a new
  patient form, i.e., insurance information, social security
  number, driver's license number, etc.

- *Medical History:* Record the names, addresses, and
  telephone numbers of all doctors related to your case.
  Also include all the treatment programs you have been
  on and any reactions or side effects suffered from
  treatment or medications.

- *Appointments:* Schedule new appointments. Record
  questions for the doctor and instructions from the
  doctor.

- *Reading:* Record the names of magazines and articles
  suggested by doctors, family, and friends.

- *Contacts:* Names and addresses of new acquaintances;
  people you meet in the doctor's office; services you may
  need.

- *Suggestions:* Other health sources suggested, i.e., second opinions, alternative and additional treatment and services.

- *Acknowledgments:* Record of gifts and other kindnesses received.

- *Addresses:* Frequently called names, addresses, and telephone numbers; your automobile club for car trouble; school phone numbers if you are delayed; neighbors' numbers for picking up children in emergencies, your spouse's work number.

WRITING OUT YOUR FEELINGS

> *"When my marriage of twenty-two years broke up, I was plunged into mental and emotional anguish. I needed more than what I was getting from psychotherapy. I began writing my feelings — continuously — clipboard in hand. Writing proved to be my lifeboat back to sanity. Later, writing became my career. . . ."*
>
> LaVada Weir, author of
> "Write Your Life Story." Instructor,
> San Pedro, California

Expressing your emotions is immensely therapeutic, and a very personal way of doing so is to write them down. Some refer to this writing technique as "journaling." You can, of course, get much the same results by using other techniques, such as drawing, playing a musical instrument, or talking into a tape recorder. Being aware of your emotions is very important in regaining health and remaining healthy. Putting your emotions down on paper, into art, or into song allows those uptight feelings and pain to be expressed.

There are numerous adult courses and books on journaling and art therapy where you can learn more about these forms of self-expression. Proposed here are some simple ways to express yourself and rid yourself of emotions and pent-up feelings. As in peeling an onion, as you remove each thin layer of emotion, the underlying layers begin to surface.

Writing On A Daily Basis

Begin by picking up a pen or pencil and writing down your feelings in a notebook. Your notes are for your eyes only, so be as expressive as you want.

Buy an appointment book, or a daily log, and keep it in a place where you will be reminded to use it daily. If you drive somewhere regularly, the glove compartment in your car is a good place to keep your book. You can then begin the habit of sitting in your car for a few minutes each day to write out your feelings. If you keep it next to your bed, you can jot down the highlight of your day and any emotions that went along with them before going to sleep. Since you will be the only one reading this log, you can abbreviate and use symbols for many of your thoughts.

Some days may be busier than others. On busy days, write only a line or two; but make that contact with your diary every day!

Certain days will be more difficult than others. On especially challenging days, take the time to write down your emotions and feelings. Often you will gain insights into your problems through this process.

ALTERNATIVES TO WRITING

Typing

A computer or typewriter is a useful tool for expressing thoughts and feelings quickly. Many people use their computer daily to make up and check on their "To Do" list. They also do their journaling on their personal computer. Those who use their typewriter daily in offices may want to express their thoughts on paper and keep them in a folder in their desk.

Voice Dialogue

Using a tape recorder to record your current feelings may be your preference. Be sure to number the tapes, and when they are full, keep them in a shoe box or similar place and file them in order. You may never want to listen to them again, but they may come in handy for reference. I know a man who has accumulated over twenty-two tapes. He started talking into his tape machine when he was told his father had cancer, and so important has this personal therapy been that he hopes to write a book about his reflections some day. If you choose not to keep your tapes, you can tape over the same one every day. The important thing to remember, however, is the process, not necessarily the product.

Art Therapy

Many people I know are able to express themselves artistically and get great emotional release in this fashion. Purchase a large artist's pad or book, obtain the paints and brushes, and begin to express your feelings. Colors can reflect changes in your personality and emotions. You can also relate your feelings in words next to the painting. I have known some people who do this writing with the opposite hand, i.e., if they are right-handed, they use their left hand to print or write a few words describing their feelings — thus activating the other side of the brain. (For more information on this idea refer to *Drawing on the Right Side of the Brain,* by Betty Edwards, Los Angeles: Jeremy Tarcher, 1979.) Crayons or magic markers are more convenient mediums that can be used with a small notebook if you prefer. Don't be afraid to express yourself through stick people or cartoon-type characters. Perfection is not what you are after, but rather the release of your emotions through art.

RESEARCH

Initially, you may feel you want more information about your illness or condition than the doctor has given you. There are various avenues that lead to such information, and you can always check with your doctor if the information you find isn't clear or needs amplification.

Books

Library: Visit your library and ask for pamphlets and medical bulletins related to your illness. Reading one book will get you started and guide you toward others. You might prefer to skim the books and pick out the ones containing information that applies to you. Check the bibliography at the end of books and the card and computer files also. The librarian will be happy to help you in your search.

Two words of caution! Remember, whatever you read in books may be history. Many advances are made daily in the field of medicine and research. Often new techniques and advances are reported in newspapers and journals before they are either proven safe to use or available. You may want to check the copyright dates on the books you are reading to ensure that the medical information is up-to-date. Many libraries have books on cassettes that you can borrow and listen to. You can also rent or buy books on tape.

Check for information on the side effects of the drugs you are taking. After all, it's your life and your body. Don't give all the responsibility of caring for it to another. Your research on the illness, the effects of your treatment, and steps you can take play an important role in your recovery.

In addition to reading about your illness, you may want to invest time and energy on the new set of challenges related to your illness. Books and articles on skin care, hair styles, and head wraps to cover hair loss or scars from surgery are helpful. There are many books on a variety of exercises and nutrition. Find one that fits your physical needs.

Books and Cassettes of New Interests: Books and tapes on starting a new hobby — calligraphy, woodwork, astronomy, cooking and so on — may help motivate you into action. Audio and audiovisual cassettes are helpful in assisting you with meditation, visualization techniques, and relaxation techniques.

CLASSES

Adult schools and community colleges offer classes on many subjects. Look through their catalogs and sign up for a class that looks interesting or, especially, one that will assist you in reaching maximum health.

TELEVISION

Television offers numerous programs on exercise, yoga, and aerobic and relaxation exercises. Several programs on nutrition and health are offered that you may want to incorporate into your lifestyle.

SUPPORT GROUPS

> *"Recovering from my son's suicide, I have
> learned that reaching out and helping others
> by sharing my own experiences is so helpful.
> Daily, I help people in support groups going
> through a life crisis. Caring and understand-
> ing seems to be what helps the most."*
> Toni Sargent, Director of Adolescent/
> Youth Bereavement Program, Facilitator of
> Survivors after Suicide, Los Angeles
> Suicide Prevention Center, Div. of
> Family Services, Los Angeles

Support groups create a safe environment for anyone
dealing with an illness. Attending one gives you an opportunity to interact with others in similar circumstances.

You will find comfort in knowing that others share
your feelings and fears. Support groups use group sessions
for the expression of feelings. Members of these groups
discuss both their mental and physical problems. They
verbalize their feelings to others who can genuinely relate to
them. A husband, a wife, a parent, or a child may be
sympathetic and caring, but they cannot understand your
deeply rooted fears and emotions. Only someone with the
same problem can be truly empathic.

Check with your hospital and doctor's office or call the
toll free information number 1-800-555-1212 and give them
the name of the organization you want to contact. The 800
number for the American Cancer Society is 1-800-4-CAN-

CER. Other 800 numbers are: AIDS Support 1-800-342-2437, Alzeheimer's Information 1-800-621-0379, and Coping with Strokes 1-800-553-6321. Many organizations have local support groups in your area.

SPECIAL EQUIPMENT NEEDS

If you are in need of special equipment for your recovery, the above support groups or local chapters will assist you. Many other organizations assist in the needs of people reaching for recovery — churches, civic organizations, and so on.

PLAN AHEAD

Make your "to do" list, then prioritize the list. Check the items to which you want to give immediate attention. No matter how insignificant an item on your list, it is important that you do it. Don't procrastinate.

The next step is to write, next to the item, how you plan to go about accomplishing the task. For example, if you are looking for certain information, call the library/book store.

You may need time to rest during the day, and if the telephone bothers you, purchase an answering machine. You can also buy a sign, "Daytime Sleeper — Do Not Disturb," to keep people from knocking on the door.

There will be days when you will not want to do anything. Take a day off. Remember the song in *Annie* — "The Sun Will Come Up Tomorrow." You will find there will be more good days than there are bad. Make time for yourself, hibernate, or listen to music.

On days you would like a focus, an important first step is to make a list of what you want to do. Utilizing the daily "To Do" list will help you be organized and focus on what you want to accomplish. It's great to refer to the list when you feel overwhelmed or depressed.

If your doctor gives you upsetting news, look for an alternative route! Get second, third, and fourth opinions. If a certain treatment is required, accept it and see what you can do to turn it into a more positive experience. It may be as simple as buying yourself a new warm-up suit to wear for the treatments so you will feel special, or buying new bed sheets for your bed (or at least new pillowcases, maybe even a favorite cartoon pillowcase character).

In spite of difficulties, rise above them. It is all in your attitude. You may want to read books about people who have been an inspiration to others. Albert Schweitzer suffered from a thirty-year stomach ailment and still carried on with his work.

SPIRALING UPWARDS

Life is an ascending spiral. Since the day we were born we have been adding to our lives. We learned to walk, to talk, to eat, and, hopefully, we never stop learning. You are at a new stage in your life now, and you will be learning new ways to enjoy it.

We constantly make changes in our wardrobe by adding new items and accessories; we do the same in our homes as we rearrange furniture and decorate for various holidays. The same applies to our diet and eating patterns. Over the years our tastes have changed. When we are enjoying a buffet, we constantly make choices. We rarely eat every-thing offered.

Now, at this new crossroad, we are making new choices. It is most important to allow newness to come into your life. It will be important to be open to the reality of new ideas. These new steps may include taking a daily nap or letting go of a few commitments so that you can take care of yourself. Do it! You are worth it! You are special! This is the only life you have. It's not a dress rehearsal. Knowledge, under-standing, love, joy, and peace will help you enlarge your outlook on life. Turn your liabilities into assets instead of just coping with what life has handed you.

IMPROVE THE QUALITY OF YOUR LIFE

Don't forget to stop on your new highway and refresh yourself with a reward. It is important that you reward yourself for the good work you are doing. Acknowledging yourself each step of the way is important. Take time out to walk in your garden or in a park. Go out and treat yourself.

Make the most of each moment. To dwell on memories of the past or visions of future possibilities is often to miss the opportunity to experience life fully in the present moment. To walk quickly past a rose bush is to miss its intense beauty and lovely scent. Learn to "stop and smell the roses." Yes-terday they were only buds, tomorrow they will be wilted, today they are in full bloom.

Begin right now to be the person you want to be. Think, feel, and behave as that person. Eliminate from your life all that is not useful or that is not compatible with your ideals. Live your life fully from this moment on.

If your goal is to write a book, but you feel too weak to sit at a desk, use a tape recorder and have someone transcribe it for you. Remember — *you* must take the first step. You are the master of your destiny! You have as much access to information and to the principles of fulfillment as does anyone else. What you are willing to do with the information you acquire and the principles you know are the determining factors.

MY EXPERIENCE

Once I chose the positive, I needed to focus on and plan the steps I was going to take. In all honesty, I often had doubts. But I persisted in reaching toward the goals I really wanted to accomplish.

There are various systems I use in reaching these goals. I started with a wish list. I found a creative technique called mind-mapping or clustering that worked for me.

MIND-MAPPING

A mind map is a pattern of connected ideas. Making one is similar to diagraming a sentence and is often referred to as clustering. The main purpose of a mind map is to bring forth your dreams and ideas, to activate both sides of the brain. A carefree approach is more fun as well as rewarding.

Begin with a focus word on a large sheet of paper and put that word in the center. Branch out from that word with all the ideas about that particular item that come to your mind. Don't worry about the order or being neat. In fact, the more open you are, the more ideas will come out of your head. Let your creative juices flow!

Following is an illustration using HEALTH as the central idea. I jotted down all the ideas that came to me regarding that subject and I let it flow.

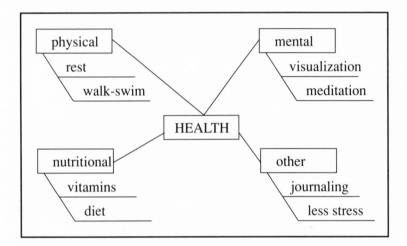

GOALS

You might prefer to set up your mind maps in an organized fashion using goals (long and short term). The following list contains some goals that I have set for myself. As you can see, when you begin setting long-term goals, you immediately create short-term goals.

Several formats can be used to set up your goals. It is a good idea to have a schedule and steps to follow for realizing them.

Long-term goal: Travel to Great Britain

Short-term goal: (steps to take to achieve long-term goal)
- Visit travel agent; get brochures
- Enroll in class on travel to Great Britain (slide and lecture series)
- Take cooking class on English Meals or buy a Great Britain cookbook and experiment
- Read magazines about the country
- Visit library; borrow books about the country
- Rent videos pertaining to Great Britain

Long-term goal: Start a new hobby that will take time to complete, i.e., building a child's doll house

Short-term goal: Building doll furniture
- Buying plans
- Visit hobby and craft shops

Long-term goal: Learn how to do calligraphy

Short-term goal: Sign up for calligraphy class
- Visit stationery/art supply store
- Practice, practice, practice
- Design your own cards

Long-term goal: Attend Art Classes

Short-term goal: Try various types of art: sketching, water-
colors, oils, etc. to see what is of interest before investing in equipment

Long-term goal: Learn about astronomy

Short-term goal: Visit planetariums
  • Enroll in astronomy class
  • Read astronomy magazines
  • Invest in good binoculars/telescope
  • Join local astronomy club

PERSONAL GOALS

Long-term goal: Improve Image/Lifestyle

Short-term goal: Try new hair style or hair piece
  • Exercise
  • Research magazines
  • Take classes
  • Purchase clothes to match lifestyle

Long-term goal: Create mental stimulation

Short-term goal: Read books
  • Practice visualization
  • Sign up for class of new interest

Long-term goal: Plan family home needs

Short-term goal: Hire someone or ask for help with housework and gardening
* Arrange meals in advance or with family and friends.

Long-term goal: Work on better relationships

Short-term goal:
* Discuss feelings with family
* Write letters to express your feelings for those you are
unable to communicate with easily
* Update photo albums together

EXPANDING YOUR WORLD

In addition to collecting all the information you can on
your recovery, it is important to do things that are not related
to your illness. In this way, you keep balance in your life.

For instance, take a class for fun and leisure that is
unrelated to health. Follow through on something you have
always wanted to do but have been postponing, or look
through a schedule of courses and take something entirely
new that appeals to you.

Sign up for a lesson in something you have always
wanted to try, i.e., tennis, golf, or flying. Let your new
interest be your focus, not your illness. You can support
these lessons by reading books, viewing videos, and watching
movies on the subject. While taking these course subjects,
don't mention your illness. I don't mean that you should

keep it secret, but don't walk into class and tell people. It may be a welcome change to go some place on a regular basis and not have to explain your personal problems and give an up-to-date report. This idea is great for both care-giver and care-receiver. You both need a break from the day-to-day routine, and you will look forward to this welcome change.

Another technique that worked for me was the "treasure map," the making of which helped me get focused on my future, and it was fun preparing it.

TREASURE MAP

A treasure map is a visual affirmation, a wish list in picture form. The art form is known as collage — small pictures pasted on paper or tacked on poster board.

The easiest way to begin making a treasure map is to make a list of things you have always wanted to do, perhaps to accomplish, make or own. Keeping your list in mind, look through various magazines and newspapers and cut out the pictures or words that describe your ideas. When you have accumulated a goodly number, paste these items on a sheet of poster board. Your treasure map can be any size. I used a large-size poster.

Building a treasure map is a wonderful experience. It will take time, but the rewards are worth it. You may want to include photographs of yourself on your board. Or cut up some photos of yourself so that your face can be superimposed over another picture. You can also edit your map by putting your name over a name in the picture. For example, tape your name over that of a person sitting in a director's chair, or put your name on the side of a car, truck, or van from a business you would like to start. Since this is your own personal treasure map, be creative and add whatever you like. Do your own artwork; print your own captions. The effort is very therapeutic and rewarding.

Perhaps sketching or drawing your treasure map will provide an even greater sensitivity and awareness. Your own drawings, no matter how primitive, are a direct reflection of your feelings, loves, desires, hopes, dreams, fears, and ambitions. A "self-drawn" montage serves a psychological purpose; it is a "concrete" expression of the "inner you."

The treasure map can also serve as a plan of the things you want to have and experience in your life. On my treasure map, I first outlined at least five areas of my life where I wanted improvement — in health, relationships, a published book, travel, and abundance. Under each of the titles, I listed exactly what I wanted. The result was something like this:

HEALTH

- Complete recovery with no reoccurrence from cancer
- Slim, trim, healthy body
- Balanced life; reduced stress
- Mentally creative in all areas

RELATIONSHIPS

Husband

- Committed relationship to husband
- Time to share our dreams and daily happenings

Children

- Special quality time with each of my children
- Get to know each child as an individual
- Take walks with them and talk about whatever subject comes up
- Visit a museum, a play, or a movie they want to see Listen to their dreams, challenges, and desires

Relatives

- Keep in contact with family on a regular basis — use the phone, letters, or postcards
- Send thoughtful gifts or news articles that interest them

Friends

- Invite friends to lunch at home, restaurant or picnic
- Enjoy being with them
- Share a cup of tea or coffee together
- Go for a walk together

- Remember them not only on birthdays but throughout the year. If a special news article would be of interest to them, cut the item out and mail it with a post-it note saying "thinking of you" (if time doesn't permit a longer letter)

WRITING A BOOK

- Write all chapters for the book
- Complete editing
- Seek a publisher
- Visualize a book signing tour and your book on store shelves

TRAVEL

- Make a list of countries and places you want to visit
- Get brochures from travel agents
- Research countries and places of interest in the library
- Take courses pertaining to the country: language, customs, cooking, or dance
- Check travel section of newspaper for information about special rates and things to do

ABUNDANCE

- Go window-shopping
- Try on different outfits. Just for fun try a different style
- Update your present wardrobe with accessories

- Visit automobile showrooms and get brochures
- Sit in car; get the feel and smell of it
- Research magazines/books on that particular model

The following are some of the words and pictures in magazine advertisements that I cut out to illustrate the various areas of my life that I wanted to improve. (You will be surprised to find the positive words used in advertising.)

HEALTH

Words:
- Comeback from Cancer
- Living Well is the Best Revenge
- Healthy Cook
- Dare to Be More
- Improve Your Shape
- Improve Your Mind and Mood

Pictures:
- Person in hammock (less stress)
- Person hang-gliding (soaring to greater heights)
- Clown juggling balls (balance in my life)
- Swimmer in pool (exercise)
- Trim lady in bathing suit

RELATIONSHIPS

Husband

Words:
*   The quality of caring
*   This man cares for me
*   Cuddle-up

Pictures:
*   Man and woman dancing in formal clothes
*   Couple walking on beach
*   Couple in mountain cottage
*   Candlelight dinner with couple
*   Airplane (couple traveling)

Children

Words:
*   Better parent-teen communication
*   You are fantastic
*   Let's eat out
*   Family strengths

Pictures:
*   Family skiing
*   Mother, father, two children enjoying vacation
*   Family eating out, having fun
*   Mother and son talking

Relatives

Words:
- Keep in touch
- I just called to say, "I love you"
- Thanks for the great gift

Pictures:
- Mother on telephone (contact with family)
- Woman writing a letter
- Lady shopping for cards and gifts
- Dad fishing in the lake

Friends

Words:
- Friends make all the difference
- Enjoy yourself
- Laughing

Pictures:
- Friends enjoying a brisk walk
- Enjoying lunch with a friend
- Biking with a companion

BOOK

Words:
- Equip yourself with the tools for success
- The power of a singular vision
- What have you accomplished today

Pictures:
- Author at book signing party
- Woman working at a computer
- Reading a best seller

TRAVEL

Words:
- Egypt and the Nile
- Alaska
- Great Britain
- Africa

Pictures:
- The Nile
- Railroad scene through Alaska
- Changing of the guard in London
- Safari clothes

ABUNDANCE

Words:
- Within Reach
- More for Your Money
- Lottery Winner

Pictures:
- Play money, $1,000 and $100 bills
- Lottery ticket with winner written on it
- Photograph of you in front of a new car

CREATIVITY

Words:
- Maybe it is that simple
- A good idea gets better
- Just do it
- Choose to make a difference

Pictures:
- Decorating a room
- Teaching in a classroom
- Writing at a desk (new ideas)

This is not only rewarding but a very therapeutic project. It reveals areas wherein you can expand your life. You are taking charge, and it only requires a seed of an idea, some scissors, tape, paper, and paste.

SUMMARY

- Don't let your thoughts overwhelm you.
- Keep a compact record or logbook.
- Keep your logbook up-to-date.
- Keep your logbook handy at all times.
- Use your logbook as a focal point for your feelings.
- Let your logbook become your security blanket.
- Express your emotions in writing.
- Make a habit of writing out your emotions each day.
- Take along a tape recorder or someone to take notes when you visit the doctor.

- Make a verbal recording of your feelings and emotions.
- Release your emotion through artistic expression.
- Research your illness.
- Take classes related to your illness.
- Enroll in a support group.
- Plan ahead.
- Remain open to change and personal growth.
- Take time to smell the roses.
- Make the most of each day and each opportunity.
- Set goals and reach for them.
- Expand your world — don't allow illness to become your whole life.
- Create a treasure map of things you want for the future.
- Map out ways for obtaining the things in your treasure map.

Reach Out to Others

CHAPTER VI

DEALING WITH FAMILY, FRIENDS, AND DOCTORS

"Even with illness you still belong to the healthy world like a stranger belongs to humanity. Don't hide. Open your arms and your mind to receive what you need. You will comfort those who give to you, and you will create a chain of goodwill, warmth, and gratitude, which every human being dreams."

Dr. Guy David
Paris, France

After I was first told that my illness was life-threatening, my perception of the reaction of those around me when they learned this was so blurred by my own emotional state, I was unable to assess what they were feeling.

Now I know that just within my family, the emotional toll the news took was heavy, and that individual reactions varied from denial to overprotectiveness, tinged by fear. My own confusion and fear were so great at first that I wasn't sure how I wanted my family to react. All I knew was that none of them behaved quite the way I thought they would, and I felt a sense of vague disappointment. Later, I learned that their reaction had nothing to do with my disappointment. I was uneasy because, unconsciously, I was beginning to face that the only person in the world who could help me and make things better was me. Even though my family might be desperately anxious to change the doctor's verdict and the way I was handling it, they were powerless.

Unconsciously, my husband knew this. There may be nothing more frustrating than the inability to help someone dear to you. The spouse bears a heavy burden when this kind of illness strikes his mate. He or she can even wish that he were the victim so he didn't have to face the numbing worry of being unable to take the necessary steps to help his loved one recover.

I believe it takes time before the ill person can appreciate what the person closest to him is going through. You will eventually have to face that very often your family fails to interact with you the way you (at that moment) feel they should. Everyone involved, unfortunately, is on a perilous emotional seesaw. You cannot and should not hide that you are dangerously ill from those who love you even though they may be as bewildered and frightened as you. Only through finding your own path to positive thinking and fighting your own fear, depression, and anger can you reassure those who love you and, in the process, improve the quality of life for everyone involved. When your emotional outlook is better, theirs will improve accordingly.

Meanwhile, purely on the practical side, you will need to be aware of the strain in terms of time and energy your condition may be putting on those close to you.

When I first told my family of my illness, my sons were eleven and fourteen years old. I wanted to shelter them from the word "cancer" that I now realize I was denying and fearful of. I explained to them that cancer was like a cavity in a tooth. You had to have it removed and everything would be all right. But, within me, I had a need to help them become self-sufficient as soon as possible in case something did happen to me. They both cooked one dinner a week and learned to do their own laundry. I told them I wanted them to be ready for survival at college. But that was only partly true. I was really afraid of dying.

A friend had forewarned me not to expect too much from any one particular family member — that they would be dealing with their own individual fears and emotions. It didn't take long for me to realize that the children were first fearful of their futures. I shared with them our family plans in the event anything was to happen to either their father or me or both of us. Addressing their fears in an open dialogue and asking them if they had any questions, eased much tension and anxiety for all of us. It gave me a chance to verbalize my concerns and comforted me not to be carrying all this anxiety inside.

Chores that were difficult for me to do became a family issue, and I did not like being in the position of "nagging" or "begging" to get things done. We had a family meeting and discussed the possibility of hiring someone to help with the cleaning. This would have to be worked into the family budget that was presently being strained with medical bills. We agreed to cut our family vacation time from two weeks to one week, hire someone every other week to help with the housework, and make other adjustments. There are still times I feel I shouldn't spend our money that way, but I am reminded that it is a mental-health investment also.

Your family and friends will respond to the news of your illness in different ways. Some will not be able to do enough for you. In extreme cases, this can be frustrating and an additional burden to you if you have a spouse or a child who is overly anxious and wearing himself out in an effort to attend to your needs. If that happens, you might have to say that you are enormously grateful for all that is being done, but it makes you feel worse to watch others exhausting themselves in your behalf, and you don't want to have to worry about them, too. The trouble is that their anxiety is catching, and you need to tell them that you would both be better thinking about more positive things. Others have difficulty knowing what to say or do, and therefore do nothing. Your husband, a grown child, or your closest friend may react this way simply because they are paralyzed by the fact of your illness and unable to come to grips with it.

I have been in both positions of Care Giver, one who attends to the needs of another, and Care Receiver, one who is the recipient of the care.

CARE GIVER

"When my eight year old daughter's
lymphoma cancer reoccurred, I was in shock.
. . . My son was the bone marrow donor. It
felt like I was in another world but one that
coexisted with everyone else's world. I was
torn. . . . I was living in the hospital with my
daughter and worried about my family at
home. My daughter's nurses told me I needed
to take time for myself and ordered me out of
the hospital for at least one hour a day.
During this hour I took a walk, checked into
a motel, did some exercise, and took a shower.
I was surprised that such a simple thing
helped me in coping. It is important for a
Care Giver to take time for herself."

Carol Ross
Rolling Hills Estates, California

When my husband had his first heart attack, I wanted
to take care of him completely. When he returned home
from the hospital, all of his meals were prepared according
to all of the heart patient cookbooks. The children were told
not to upset their father for any reason, and whenever I
awoke at night I checked to see if he was breathing. It is
necessary to add here that these were not his requests but my
needs, and I was exhausted. Whenever someone called they
asked how he was feeling? He was getting plenty of rest and
improving every day. I was growing more and more tired.

Five years later he had a second heart attack. This was after my experience with cancer, and I realized I didn't have to do it all. It was important for me to take care of myself so I could take care of him. When neighbors and friends called and offered to help, I accepted. Several of his coworkers wanted to visit, and we arranged times for their visit. It was a two-fold blessing. I could do the shopping or treat myself to time alone, and it gave my husband a chance to talk of work or sports without including me.

> Choosing to help friends in this way is no easy undertaking. When you feel stretched to breaking just keeping your own life going, it is difficult to extend your energies further to make others feel at ease. It can be a new and difficult experience for some, this reaching out, but the rewards can be exhilarating. We all feel better giving than receiving so it might be easier if you think of your requests for assistance as letting others feel useful, rather than as petitions for help. (*Taking Time*, p. 41. National Institute of Health Publication No.83-2059, reprinted 1983.)

Both the Care Giver and Care Receiver need to know that no one can do it all. We each have certain areas wherein we can assist the patient and feel comfortable doing so.

ROLE OF CARE GIVER

Family and friends often want to help in any way possible. Many of us feel we don't know "how" or "what" to do for the patient. You as the Care Giver need to be comfortable with the patient and aware of your own and the patients's feelings.

Family members and friends can serve in different roles. You might listen as the patient expresses feelings, or you might act as a sounding board for discussion of future plans. You can help patients focus anger or anxiety by exploring with them the specific causes of their anger, such as drug reactions, job situations, or finances. Someone to listen to, to react to, and to absorb the patient's outpouring may be just what is needed. It is a difficult role, but it can be immensely rewarding.

Care Givers must also remember to take care of themselves so that they can take care of others. The wear and tear of trying to do everything can be draining and can lead to ill health for the Care Giver.

Most phone calls and cards ask about the patient's well-being, but Care Givers need a pat on the back once in a while as well. Reward yourself by getting out and giving yourself time free of responsibility for all the time and effort you lovingly give the patient.

Keep open the lines of communication between the patient and your own personal support group. Invite the patient to participate in decision-making processes and talk about the areas in which he feels capable of participating regarding his own care. Also discuss the areas where you can assist or get outside help.

SUGGESTIONS

There are many ways for your family and friends to help you, and they are not limited to giving flowers and candy. The most precious gift is a gift of time.

The following suggestions help Care Givers be of maximum benefit to the patient by making his life easier.

NETWORKING

Meals:

A close friend or family member can organize a calendar for meals, using volunteer help. Schedule meals so that a meal can be brought by a volunteer. The meal donors should call the coordinator for a convenient date and time to make a meal delivery, for meal preferences, and for any diet restrictions. It is not necessary to be a gourmet cook when preparing meals. In fact, patients might not be able to handle rich or heavy foods that are difficult to digest because of medications. Ask if there are any spices or foods they do not like or cannot eat. Also, consider that they are in a healing mode and usually unable to exercise. Donors should mark dishes or use disposable trays. Also indicate cooking or heating instructions.

Housework:

Offer to help clean up, even if just for one hour. Vacuuming makes a home look picked up. Changing the bed linens makes the patients feel better, and they will think about you when they lie in bed that evening. Cleaning the windows can brighten the patient's outlook (you don't have to volunteer to do the whole house).

Sewing:

Many times, due to surgery or physical restrictions, clothing needs to be modified to fit specific requirements.

Gardening:

Mowing and watering a lawn, planting a few flowers or plants, and caring for house plants are most helpful.

Laundry/Ironing:

Take laundry/ironing to your home, or do the laundry/ ironing in the patient's home. You might also pick up and deliver clothes from the cleaners or laundromat.

Time:

Offer a few hours of your time to assist the patient. For example, write a letter that the patient dictates to you or read to them.

Shopping:

Volunteer for long or short trips to the market. Weekly shopping or even an occasional phone call to see if you can pick up a "surprise" is a nice gesture and will cheer up the patient. It is helpful if the patient keeps an ongoing grocery list and keeps money or a checkbook nearby to pay for groceries.

Get prescriptions filled, and pick up other medical needs. You might also pick up materials at a hardware store, things that will assist in the patient's new lifestyle. Shop for necessary clothing needs or pick up orders placed to medical supply houses.

Be sure to shop for the patients' requests. Even though a person is ill, life still goes on around them. The patient may still want to give gifts for birthdays and anniversaries. Offer to take the patient shopping on these occasions so that their illness does not make them feel out of the mainstream. If their strength does not permit shopping, offer to shop for them, keeping in mind their personal choices and suggestions.

Pick up favorite foods or a treat. If you know her favorite salad dressing at a special restaurant, surprise her with it.

Transportation

Offer to drive patients to their doctors' appointments or therapies. Take them to their hairdresser or barber. Take the children to school, scouts, camp, lessons, and ball games, or drive them to church/synagogue for a service or counseling. Offer to drive to an entertainment (for a short car ride to look at a view, to go out to eat, to a movie, the library, the theater, or a class).

Take them to the post office or the bank or pick up deposit/withdrawal slips to be conveniently prepared at home.

Gifts

A nice treat to look forward to is going out for breakfast, lunch or dinner, or even for tea with friends. Such an outing provides a change of scenery and adds variety to the patient's life. Pick a time when restaurants are less crowded to avoid waiting in lines.

Pick up and return rental movies and VCR, or pick up and return books from the library. Send a videotape of family/friends or have old family movies or slides made into videotapes. You can send audio tapes of a recorded message or of music they enjoy. Write letters or send cards on a regular basis. You might write letters dictated by the patient to his friends or business acquaintances, or perhaps organize a group of people (or have an organization plan this) to donate small gifts sometimes called a Sunshine Basket. Put all wrapped gifts in a fancy basket. Place a small tag on the basket with a little poem such as:

> "A little gift of sunshine
> along the way. . . .
> Open only one gift
> to brighten each day."

Or you may merely wish to sit and reminisce together.

Simplifying the Patients' Environment

If the patient is incapacitated, a bell or an intercom is useful for summoning help. Cordless intercoms are available that plug into the wall of any room. Automatic telephone dialers work with the simple push of a button.

Next to a favorite chair or bed, place a little basket that holds small items the patient might need, such as a note pad and pen, telephone book, TV remote control, eyeglasses, nail file, and a scissors for clipping news or magazine articles. This basket can be moved with the patient to wherever they are in the house.

Organize cleansing needs in one box and keep it handy so the patient can assist himself/herself with personal needs. The box would contain dental needs, tissues, deodorant, creams, a razor, a small mirror, and so on.

CARE RECEIVER

Before my two surgeries for cancer, whenever I had been hospitalized, I found it very difficult to receive help from others. I felt I could manage and didn't want to trouble anyone. Even after the first cancer surgery I didn't want anyone to know I had cancer. I was denying it to myself, and I told very few others. This meant I did not reach out and ask for help.

My second surgery took more of a toll on me. I had arrived at the hospital exhausted from all the planning before the operation; arranging the children's schedule, preparing and freezing dinners, and trying to do it all. The surgery this time was extensive and required a longer hospitalization. I soon learned that I had a wonderful support system. The "word" got out that I had cancer. A network of friends surfaced with calls to take the children, prepare meals, and even scrub floors. I soon realized that when help was offered, a simple "thank you" was all that was needed.

> There is no doubt that being sick brings with it
> the wish to be passive and to be taken care of.
> When you're sick, you have permission to let
> go of your daily pressures and obligations
> while your body takes time to heal and your
> mind takes time to adjust to the changes that
> illness can bring to your life. Ironically, as we
> let go of one set of obligations from our usual
> role in society, we assume another series of
> "have-to's" and "should's" in the form of the
> patient role. Pressure from doctors, from the
> hospital staff and from your family can add a
> new sense of burden. (Neil A. Fiore, *The Road
> Back To Health*, New York: Bantam. 1984).

As the patient, you may have to adjust your regularly active schedule while you are healing. But even as you readjust your daily routine, a new set of commitments as a patient will surface. Coping with new responsibilities often adds stress to our lives, and stress is to be avoided during the healing process. Family and friends make up a network that is ready to support you, and they are essential in maintaining a balance in your life.

Reach out to your friends. When a friend says "Call me if I can help," don't end the interaction with "Thank you for caring." They are sincere, yet helpless. Call them! and say, "I went to my therapy today and am not feeling that great — could you cook double of what you are making for dinner and send some over? I'm too exhausted to cook," or ask them (or your family) to bring home some take-out foods. Such requests help your family and friends feel "involved" in your recovery. Remember, they love you, and you are helping them help you.

Some people have a very difficult time dealing with illness and death. Help these people by calling them and saying, "Hi! I haven't heard from you in a while. I thought you might like to hear that I am doing pretty well!" You can thus help others deal with their apprehensions, while at the same time, building a strong support network for yourself.

Writing Letters

A health crisis is an emotional time when our feelings and those around us need special handling. Often we have trouble communicating our feelings to others. Someone close to you can still be difficult to communicate with verbally. Writing a letter might be the best way to get your point across.

Handling emotional stress is difficult for everyone, and each of us, being unique, handles things differently. When someone doesn't appear to be hearing what you are trying to tell them, write them a letter. Communication is especially difficult when we are involved in a crisis situation and our emotions are close to the surface.

It is also helpful to write out your needs and requests, both for your doctors, regarding treatment, and for your family, regarding more personal matters.

COMMUNICATION WITH DOCTORS AND THERAPISTS

> *"Recommendations on* how to talk to your doctor *really express the needs that we all have to be our own advocates . . . to be nicely assertive so that we can help ourselves in time of crisis.*
>
> Helene Brown, Director, Community
> Applications of Research,
> Jonsson Cancer Center at UCLA

After each visit with your doctor you should leave the office with a clear state of mind. Don't leave any of your questions unanswered. Ask probing questions and get a thorough understanding of your illness and treatment. Here are some suggestions on effectively communicating with your doctor.

- Make a list of questions and bring them in written form to your next doctor's appointment.
- Ask him for an explanation of the illness you are dealing with, i.e. how it is contracted, possible treatments, etc.
- If more tests are required for evaluation, ask what the results will reveal.

- When therapies or medications are recommended, inquire about the possible side effects. Will it be painful?
- What are the costs involved? How much time will it take?
- Tell him of research you have done on your illness, new therapies, and treatments you have heard or read about. Ask your doctor to comment on them.
- Inquire about the alternatives if you elect not to have the suggested treatment.

If the doctor's answers are superficial and unclear or if his schedule does not permit enough time for the explanation, ask him to suggest someone, possibly on his staff, who can.

Often you may have heard or read something that contradicts what the doctor has told you. In cases like these it is best to communicate with the doctor by telling him what you have heard and asking his opinion. Get a good idea of the pros and cons of a particular treatment from the doctor and let him know that this will help you make the correct decision. At the end of the visit, check to be sure that all of your questions have been answered. Be perfectly clear about your treatment and any side-effects that might occur. Then, before you leave, restate your understanding of the treatment to the doctor. This allows the doctor to correct anything that you might have missed and puts the two of you on the same wavelength. Remember, you should leave the doctor's office with a clear understanding of everything the doctor said and what you have heard or read in the past.

MY EXPERIENCE

I wrote down all the available information that I could gather on my illness, most of which I obtained from researching various medical books from the library. It helped prepare me to ask the doctor's opinion and receive valuable feedback for review. Also, when I want to express my fears, get advice on my physical reactions to treatment, or to request a change in the treatment protocol, I write a letter to my doctor and pass it on to the nurse on the day of my visit and request that she ask him to read it before visiting me in the examining room.

COMMUNICATION WITH FAMILY AND FRIENDS

"I have a good friend whose son died of a drug overdose. I wanted to call her but I was at a loss for words. I sat with my hand on the phone for an hour. I finally dialed and said, 'I don't know what to say,' and I began to cry! She comforted me. She said, 'Your love and caring and the fact that you made this incredibly difficult phone call touch me deeply and I'll never forget it.' We then chatted for an hour and talked about how friendly and outgoing her son was. I have never had a problem with calling or writing anyone who suffered a loss since. That 'terrific' lady

> *taught me the value of sharing another's
> pain."*
>
> Marnel Maddox
> Stuart, Florida

Writing or typing a letter has been an excellent way for me to communicate with some of my family members who found it difficult to talk about my illness. It gave me time to complete my feelings and gave them an opportunity to read the letter and react before talking about it with me.

In fact, I have several friends who write letters often, and others who record their messages on an audio cassette and mail them to me. After listening to their message, I record on side two of the tape and mail it back to them. We can thus reminisce about old times, and often other family members get to say hello on the tape. At first it may be difficult to get used to talking to a tape recorder, but I encourage you to stick with it. The rewards are worth the effort!

REACH OUT

As the patient, you may feel powerless, for you are depending on others for your care. But learning to adjust and cope with your illness and recovery is a challenge. In fact, you are in charge of your future. Starting now, focus on your survival. List the different areas in your life where you will need help. Think of yourself as the conductor of an orchestra. You have many musicians (family and friends) who want to support you. Give them direction and guidance on how they can help make your life easier, less stressful, and more comfortable.

SUMMARY

- Be aware of how your illness affects those closest to you
- Learn how to be an effective Care Giver
- Open your heart to the good will of others as a Care Receiver
- Communicate with your Doctors and Therapists
- Share your feelings through letter and tapes

The Choice Is Yours. Take Off and Go For It

CHAPTER VII

LOOKING TOWARD
THE FUTURE

*"We must remember that all of life is a
learning experience. We grow and expand
through everything and everyone that touches
us. We must learn to use our growth to its
fullest extent. Rather than ask 'Why?,' we
should ask, 'What can I do with my experience that will be fruitful and beneficial to
others and to myself?'"*

Marnel Maddox
Stuart, Florida

You are standing at a crossroads. Behind you is your
past life, containing all your accomplishments and memo-

ries. Pause for a moment to reflect on the way your life has been to date.

Now look at the present. You are faced with new challenges, and there is a choice to be made. Two separate routes lead into the future. One road is paved with positive thinking, but choosing this road will make demands on you. It may involve viewing things in different ways, but ultimately it will bring you to more wonders and happiness and improve the quality of your life. The other road, allowing fear, depression, and anger to rule you, is paved with negativity. This is the easy path and requires no work from you. The patients who follow this path for too long become too tired and indifferent to resist.

It is up to you alone to make the decision about which path you will follow. I can only promise if you take the road of positive thinking, you will meet many wonderful people and make new friends in your search. It seems to me that at times I receive back many times more than the effort I have expended. Most of my friends have shown such generosity of spirit I can't begin to thank them enough for being so special and caring. Take notice of these special people in your life.

Decision making in itself can be draining. It can be described as being like climbing over a wall — getting to the top is rough work, but once there, you can just fall over to the other side. Following through with the decision, then, will likely be the easy part. If you do choose the positive path, you will want to get started now. The first step is the crucial one.

So first, revise your impressions about your diagnosis. Most of us cringe when we hear the word "terminal"; we can think only of endings. However, when the word is used in conjunction with other words, as in "airport terminal," or "train terminal," we think of new beginnings. We are off on a trip, a journey that may be full of surprises.

A computer terminal allows connection between several computers, the joining of many monitors and keyboards, and the word "terminal" is also defined as a connective point on an electrical circuit. This is really what you are doing — connecting your past with the newness of your future. It may be frightening but look at the possibilities rather than the endings. Revise your thinking, for your attitude affects your day-to-day living. Change your thinking and incorporate a positive outlook.

As you travel into the future, you will find many side streets and paths to detour you. Some roads will be dead-ends where you may feel stranded, others will be beautiful paths where you will meet many wonderful people. In your travels you will explore areas new to you where you can and will discover new things about yourself. You may start new hobbies and treat yourself to things you had put on hold, awaiting the proper time in your schedule.

Start making some plans. Making plans takes time and energy, but following a positive path is worth the effort. Go for it!

BIBLIOGRAPHY

American Cancer Society. *Taking Time*. National Institute of Health Publication No. 83-2059, 1983.

Benson, Herbert. *Relaxation Response*. New York: Morrow, 1975.

Cousins, Norman. *Anatomy of an Illness*. New York: Norton 1979.

Cousins, Norman. *Head First: The Biology of Hope*. New York: Dutton, 1989.

Edwards, Betty. *Drawing on the Right Side of the Brain*. Los Angeles, J. P. Tarcher, 1979.

Fiore, Neil A. *The Road Back to Health*. New York: Bantam 1984.

Holmes, Ernest and Willis Kinnear. *Thoughts Are Things*. California: Science of Mind Publications, 1967.

Padus, Emrika. *The Complete Guide to Your Emotions and Your Health*. Pennsylvania: Rodale Press, 1986.

Powers, Melvin. *A Practical Guide to Self-Hypnosis*. California: Wilshire Book Co., 1968.